Praise for *Show Your Paycheck Who's Boss*

"*Show Your Paycheck Who's Boss* is more than a how-to guide for finances. It's a how-to guide for life! I so wish this book had been around when I was a young, single mom. But like they say, better late than never!"

—Mona Andrei, Award-winning humor blogger, Author of *SUPERWOMAN: A Funny and Reflective Look at Single Motherhood*

"I so wish I would have had this easily followed instructional, *Show Your Paycheck Who's Boss,* when starting out as a young'un. I could have sorely used the author's wise envelope system from 'When the Divorce is Final,' 'Making Money Mistakes,' 'Cosigning,' and all the way through to 'Retirement.' I would be a billionaire by now, alas!"

—Parris Afton Bonds, NYT Bestselling Author

$how Your Paycheck Who's Bo$$

Diane Windsor

Published by Motina Books, LLC, Van Alstyne, Texas
www.MotinaBooks.com

Library of Congress Cataloguing-in-Publication Data:
Names: Windsor, Diane
Title: Show Your Paycheck Who's Boss – Financial Guide & Planner for Single Parents
Description: First Edition. | Van Alstyne: Motina Books, 2022

Identifiers:
LCCN: 2022943747
ISBN-13: 978-1-945060-68-7 (paperback)

Subjects: BISAC:
Non-Fiction > Personal Finance

Cover Design: Diane Windsor
Interior Design: Diane Windsor

DEDICATION

For all the single moms and single dads out there. You're killing it.

You ARE the Boss

It may feel like as soon as you get your paycheck, all the money you worked so hard to earn just flies out of your bank account. It's so incredibly frustrating! You're working your fingers to the bone and taking care of your kids. Why does it feel like you don't have any money?

The main reason that many Americans are in this situation today is because they're not intentionally managing their money and making sure that every single dollar has a specific purpose. You are the boss of your money. You need to tell it what to do, and make sure that it's behaving!

You also need to think about what your own philosophy about money. Everyone has a money philosophy. You may not be aware of it, but you do! When you think about the money you earn, what is important to you? Do you get excited when you spend your money, and bring home new clothes or something for your home? Or is it more thrilling to put money into your savings account?

Your personal money philosophy will encompass many different areas. How do you feel about debt? Are you comfortable having a car payment, student loan payment, and credit card payment? Or, do you avoid debt like the plague, and refuse to pay interest to anyone? It may even be your goal to get out of debt and build up your savings accounts. It's my goal to help you with that.

Lending and giving money to others is part of the philosophy, as well. It's very common for families to lend to and borrow from each other. As parents, we want to help our kids, right? And, what if your sister is in a bind, and needs to money to get her through the next couple of months? Of course we want to help. But, is lending money to them really helping them? Will you ever get that money back? How will a loan to a family member impact your relationship?

Everyone has a different opinion about how to handle money. On television, radio, and the Internet, there is no lack of financial advice. There are so many "experts" who want to tell you how to invest and save money. Many experts are also teaching people how to get out of debt, and how to avoid debt entirely, which is extremely valuable. If you don't have debt payments, you know what you have? Money!

Show Your Paycheck Who's Boss is a little different than other books that offer financial advice. If you're single with no kids, then you only have yourself to worry about. You buy food and clothing just for you. You can live in a teeny studio basement apartment because you don't need much room.

If you're a married couple with, or without, children, then you must be on the same page about money. The number one cause of divorce in the United States is money fights and money problems. It's vital that you both agree about the way you handle money. For example, when one person wants to make a large purchase, there needs to be a conversation and a mutual decision.

But if you're a single parent, you face a different set of hurdles than the single person with no kids, or the married couple. In this book we will address the financial issues that are specific to single parents. Single parents face money problems that other people have never even dreamed of! In this book, we're going to talk about all of them.

I used to lead a large single parent support group in the Dallas area. We focused on a variety of topics including family connection time, providing legal advice, and, of course, financial counseling. I worked with many moms and dads who had struggled financially, and were ready to start demolishing their debt and saving their money. By having a plan and sticking to that plan, this is absolutely possible.

Single parents can win with money. It won't be easy. You'll need to make sacrifices, and you'll need to be very disciplined. You have to want it more than you want that new iPhone, or that new pair of shoes. Do you get a mani-pedi every two weeks? Sorry—you'll need to reconsider that expense. Once you reach that point of being debt-free, having some money in your savings account, and being able to put money away for retirement, you'll know that all the sacrifices were worth it. You'll have the joy of knowing that you're in the relatively small percentage of people in this country who are not living paycheck-to-paycheck. You won't have to wonder how you're going to pay for a medical bill, or your child's upcoming field trip. Braces? No problem! You can do it, because you are winning with your money! You have the right money philosophy.

What Are Your Financial Goals?

☐ Pay Off Debt

☐ Grow Your Emergency Fund

☐ Save For Retirement

☐ Save for a Special Purchase

☐ Save for Education

☐ Start a Side Business

☐ Find a New Job

☐ Earn More Money in Your Current Job

Other Goals

Personal finance is just that—it's PERSONAL. What are some of your life goals, other than financial?

_____

_____

_____

_____

_____

_____

_____

_____

_____

_____

Sometimes when you're going through a divorce, you might have a lot of negative thoughts running through your mind. These may include guilt, shame, and just thinking a bit less of yourself. I certainly had these thoughts when I was getting divorced. I felt like a failure, and nothing really helped me at that time.

The planner that begins on the next page will help you see things in a more positive light.

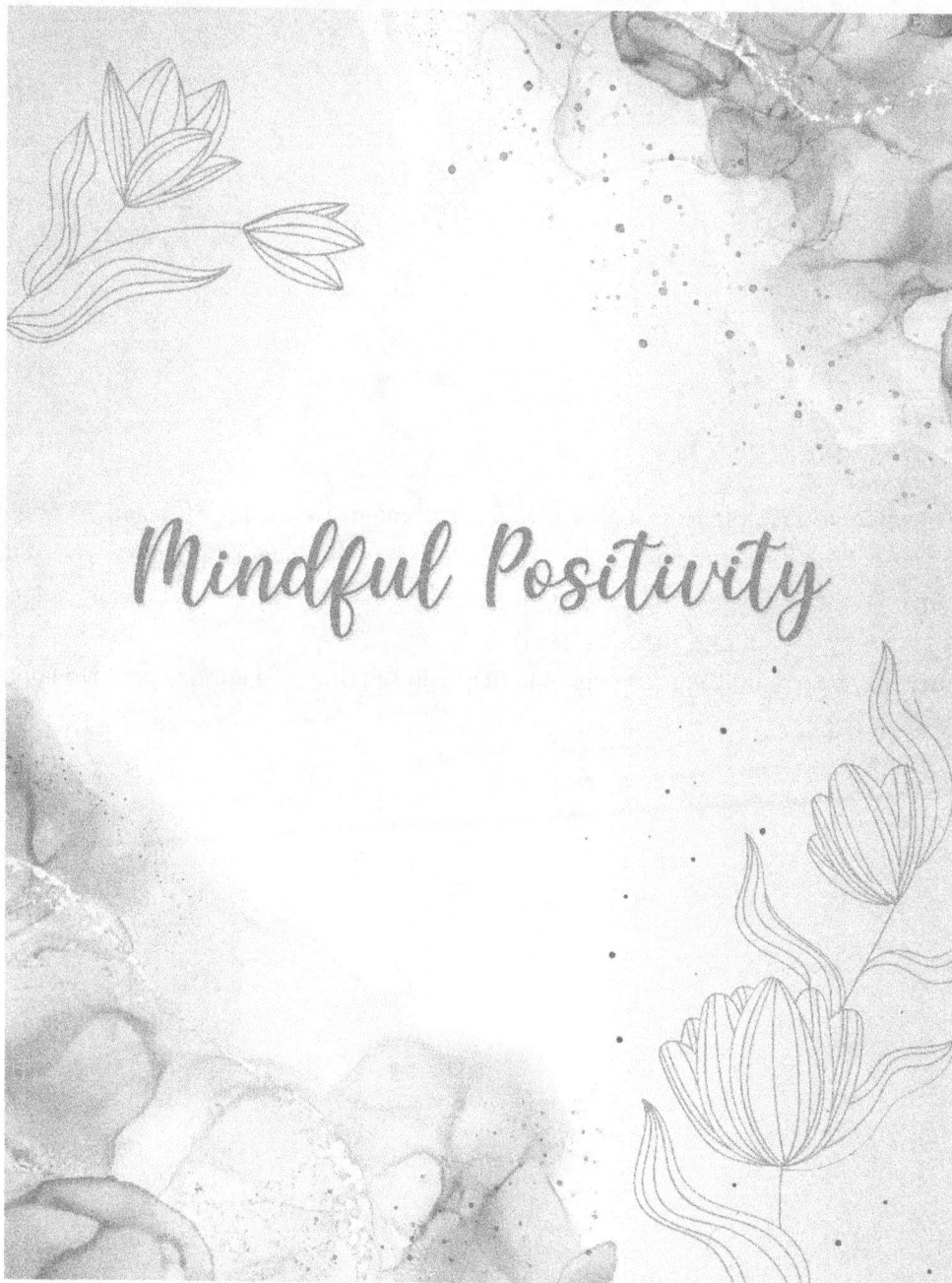

Mindful Positivity

Objectives

Positivity is something we could all use a little more of in our lives. However, without some helpful tools to keep us mindful of maintaining a positive mindset, it's hard to accomplish. The good news... since you are here, you're already well on your way to creating a more positive mindset. Let's begin by defining why and what you are hoping to achieve with this workbook.

Why do you want to be more positive?

....

....

....

....

....

....

How do you think being more positive can help you?

....

....

....

....

....

What kind of person do you want to be by the time you finish this workbook?

....

....

....

....

....

Starting The Day With Positivity

How you start your day sets the tone for the rest of your day. If you have an unpleasant morning, chances are that it will cast a shadow over your whole day. It's important to have a routine that allows you to start your day off on the right foot. Let's go over your morning routine.

How do you normally start your day?

....
....
....
....
....
....

Do you feel happy with this routine?

☐ Yes   ☐ No   ☐ Somewhat

What can you do to start your day better? Or, if you do not have a routine, create one. It doesn't have to be elaborate. A bullet list will suffice.

♡ ....
♡ ....
♡ ....
♡ ....
♡ ....
♡ ....
♡ ....
♡ ....
♡ ....
♡ ....
♡ ....
♡ ....

Gratitude

Gratitude is one foundation of a positive mindset. If you can't be thankful—even for the little things—you won't see things in a positive light. Even during difficult times, being able to find things to be grateful for can be an encouragement to hold on to. On the flip side, during good times, being mindful of gratitude is a great way to not take these times for granted. Curate a list of things you have to be grateful for.

List 5 people

....

....

....

....

....

List 5 things

....

....

....

....

....

List 5 places

....

....

....

....

....

List 5 memories

....

....

....

....

....

Anything else?

....

....

....

....

....

Improve Your Self-Image

A positive self image can help improve a lot of different aspects of your life. When you feel good about yourself, you're less likely to blame or hate yourself for things beyond your control. For example, instead of beating yourself up for a mistake, you can simply own up to that mistake, fix it if possible, and move on—without all the negative put-downs to yourself.

How do you see yourself?

....
....
....
....

Are you happy with your personality?

....
....
....
....

How do you feel about your appearance?

....
....
....
....

Do you speak to yourself with kindness?

☐ 1 (Rarely)   ☐ 2 (Sometimes)   ☐ 3 (Neither)   ☐ 4 (Frequently)   ☐ 5 (Always)

What's one step you can take to be kinder to yourself & improve your self image?

....
....
....
....

Hobbies

There's more to life than work, eat, and sleep. Hobbies bring us joy. Whether you like to cook, paint, sew, workout, clean, or go out with friends, it's important to always set some time aside for hobbies. Without hobbies, our lives just don't have that same spark of positivity and happiness. It is not selfish to pursue them. Let's make a plan to build in time for your hobbies.

What's your hobby? If you've lost touch with your hobby, what would you love to do if you have some down time?

....
....
....
....
....

Inspect your typical day and week. When are you doing mindless things, like watching TV or social media?
Look for spots to fit hobby time into your schedule.

Time	Mon	Tue	Wed	Thu	Fri	Sat	Sun
From: To:							
From: To:							
From: To:							
From: To:							
From: To:							
From: To:							

Positivity In The Workplace

It's common for people to not enjoy their work. However, if you go into it with a negative attitude, it can make it that much harder to get through the days. Finding the little things to be positive about can help you make your job a better place for you—and even the rest of your coworkers. There is always something good to see as long as you keep your eyes open.

Do you enjoy your job?

☐   ☐   ☐   ☐   ☐

1 (Not at all)   2 (Sometimes)   3 (Neither)   4 (Often)   5 (Everyday)

What about the people you work with?

☐   ☐   ☐   ☐   ☐

1 (No)   2 (A few)   3 (Some)   4 (Many)   5 (Most)

Do you often complain or join in with complaining about work?

☐   ☐   ☐   ☐   ☐

1 (Rarely)   2 (Sometimes)   3 (Neither)   4 (Frequently)   5 (Always)

List 5 positive things about.

Your job.   The people you work with.

....

....

....

....

....

What's one thing you can do to stay positive about and at work next time you go in?

....

....

....

....

....

Positivity At Home

Home should be a place where we feel comfortable, safe, and happy. (NOTE: If you are ever unsafe in your home for any reason, leave immediately, and contact your local authorities.) You may not enjoy the city you live in, or the people you live with. However, it's important to remember to be proactive with your mindset and actions.

Do you feel happy when you're at home?

☐	☐	☐	☐	☐
1 (Not at all)	2 (Sometimes)	3 (Neither)	4 (Often)	5 (Everyday)

Why don't you like being at home?

....
....
....
....
....
....
....
....
....

How can you change your perspective? Is there anything you can do?

....
....
....
....
....
....
....
....
....
....

Productivity & Procrastination

There are probably a lot of tasks that you don't want to do. But putting these things off only prolongs the feelings of negativity. You're also making things harder for yourself because you're falling farther and farther behind. Thankfully, you can foster a positive attitude around these tasks to help you get them done faster, and save you a lot of stress.

What tasks do you keep putting off?

....
....
....
....
....

What would you enjoy doing or rather be doing instead?

....
....
....
....
....

Can you pair or do them at the same time? If not, what activity is one activity you enjoy that you can pair with this task? For example, if you don't enjoy working out and would rather watch TV, then watch TV while working out.

....
....
....
....
....
....

Say Yes To Yourself

Sometimes, out of guilt, fear, or other negative emotions, we talk ourselves out of things that bring us positivity. Don't rob yourself of that opportunity. Remember that it's OKAY to say yes to yourself sometimes.

Write the times when you talk yourself out of things that would make you happy or blocked them.

....

....

....

....

....

....

Why do you do this?

....

....

....

....

One's one affirmation you can say to yourself the next time you slip into this pattern?

....

....

....

....

....

Taking On Other's Emotions

Some people can feel and take on other people's feelings. This is what's known as an Empath. It can become overwhelming if not controlled. If the negative emotions of surrounding people affect you, you'll want to learn to ground yourself. It can be anything from prayer and meditation to wearing headphones. Different tricks work for different people, so don't be afraid to be creative and let's start by making a list so you are prepared.

Grounding Tricks To Try

1. Prayer/Meditation
2. Headphones
3. 5 senses method
4. Exercise
5. Laugh
6. Stretch
7. Visualize
8.
9.
10.
11.
12.
13.
14.
15.
16.
17.
18.
19.
20.
21.
22.
23.

Holding On / Letting Go

We can keep ourselves from developing a positive mindset by holding on to negativity. Holding onto grudges, petty annoyances, or other things that don't matter in the big picture keeps you from seeing and appreciating all the good that's around you. Reflect on what kind of negativity you are holding onto, ask yourself why, and then think about how you can let go of those things.

Do you make a habit of dwelling on and holding onto negative thoughts or experiences?

☐ ---------- ☐ ---------- ☐ ---------- ☐ ---------- ☐

1 (Rarely)　　2 (Sometimes)　　3 (Neither)　　4 (Frequently)　　5 (Always)

Why do you think you do this?

_____

_____

_____

_____

_____

_____

_____

Research and write at least one thing you can remind yourself of when you feel this way.

_____

_____

_____

_____

_____

_____

_____

_____

Relationships

Unhealthy relationships can bring in a lot of negativity into your life. Unfortunately, it's difficult to weed out these types of relationships; especially if they are family or long-time friends. It's important to remember that your mental health and overall well-being should come first. If someone is constantly bringing negativity and ill intentions into your life, you may break things off with them.

Name one person who annoys you or rubs you the wrong way.

....

Write one thing you can do to distance yourself.

....

....

....

Write one thing you do or say when they annoy you. (Remember. to be positive you also want to be kind. Being nasty only builds more negative emotions later.)

....

....

....

Name one person who annoys you or rubs you the wrong way.

....

Write one thing you can do to distance yourself.

....

....

Write one thing you do or say when they annoy you. (Remember. to be positive you also want to be kind. Being nasty only builds more negative emotions later.)

....

....

....

Exercise

Exercise is not only good for your health, it can work wonders for your mental health as well. When we exercise, our bodies also release a lot of feel-good hormones that can really help us look on the bright side. Think of exercise as a kind of "reset" for your brain that will help you think more clearly and positively.

When are you doing mindless things, like watching TV or social media? Look for pockets of time to fit in some exercise. Remember, it doesn't have to be a huge hour long workout. You can take a walk for lunch or do stepping exercises while you watch TV.

Time	Mon	Tue	Wed	Thu	Fri	Sat	Sun
From: To:							
From: To:							
From: To:							
From: To:							
From: To:							
From: To:							
From: To.							
From: To:							

Eating Well

Exercise is great, but eating right is important too. A healthy body helps to create a healthier mind! What you eat can affect your emotions. Each person has their own needs and you should never go on a new diet without speaking to your doctor or licensed nutritionist. Let's make a plan to discuss this with your doctor.

List the programs you want to try or attempt.

....
....
....

List the questions for your doctor or nutritionist about this program.

....
....
....
....
....

Notes from your discussion.

....
....
....
....
....

Next steps.

....
....
....
....

Sleep Well

Without a good night's sleep, we slow your whole body down—including your brain. If you feel tired, and you can't think clearly, positive thoughts are not going to come naturally or easily. Let's develop a bedtime routine and schedule to help you get a better night's sleep.

Think about what time you want to wake up, add some room for a startup routine or time for yourself. Count backwards a minimum of 7 hours 15-30 minutes for a bedtime routine. What is your bedtime?

....

Are you going to sleep at this time or earlier?

☐ Yes   ☐ No

Earlier, when determining your bedtime, we added an extra 30 minutes for a wind down routine. Do you have one?

☐ Yes   ☐ No

If not, write a few things you can do in these 30 minutes to "close your day" and to prepare for a restful night. This can be simple things like brushing your teeth, changing into your jammies, meditating for 5 minutes.

....

....

It's easy to create a routine and bedtime. Harder to keep it. What's one thing you can do to trigger your bedtime routine above? This could be a simple alarm, or something that routinely happens around that time.

....

....

Keep yourself accountable. What happens if you do not keep your routine? Get creative and enlist the help of others. E.g. You would owe your partner a massage.

....

....

Accepting Negativity

Creating a more positive attitude does not mean that you ignore anything negative because it's part of life. It's important that while you are trying to be more positive, that you learn to accept negativity as it comes without dwelling on it.

Do you find that you are always trying to be in denial about negativity?

☐ Yes　　☐ No

Why do you think you do this?

Is that the best way to handle it?

☐ Yes　　☐ No

Instead of dwelling or ignoring it, what are some positive things you can say to yourself when you experience this type of negativity? Or how can you reframe it?

Making It A Lifelong Habit

Every day, we have opportunities to create, see, and allow positivity to happen. Now that you've put into practice some of these exercises, you have the tools to make it a lifelong habit. Let's condense these exercises into a habit guide you can use daily or when the need arises. For each item below, list 3 things you can do or say...

When you wake up

1. ....
2. ....
3. ....

When you get to work

1. ....
2. ....
3. ....

When you feel pressured

1. ....
2. ....
3. ....

When you start getting angry

1. ....
2. ....
3. ....

When you feel sad

1. ....
2. ....
3. ....

When you start dwelling on things that may or may not happen

1. ....
2. ....
3. ....

Build Your Affirmation List

Affirmations can help when you keep your eyes on the positive when you experience negative emotions or situations. Start collecting them and write them here for easy access in the future.

1. ....
2. ....
3. ....
4. ....
5. ....
6. ....
7. ....
8. ....
9. ....
10. ....
11. ....
12. ....
13. ....
14. ....
15. ....
16. ....
17. ....
18. ....
19. ....
20. ....
21. ....
22. ....
23. ....
24. ....
25. ....

When the Divorce is Final

During the years that a couple is married, they will most likely purchase a number of items together. What used to be "yours" and "mine" becomes "ours." This is especially true when a couple buys large items that require a bank loan, or when they open a joint credit card.

A court order that dissolves a marriage will usually be accompanied by a document known as a Divorce Decree, or a Separation Agreement. This document will list everything you need to do to separate your life from your ex's once the divorce is final.

It will tell both parties what they need to do in order to financially separate from each other. You want to make sure that you no longer have any joint bank accounts, credit cards, or loans together. Some of these items are easy to take care of, while others take more effort.

I cannot emphasize this strongly enough—do what the decree tells you to do. If you don't, there could be some serious consequences.

It's important to understand that just because this separation of assets was ordered by the court, you still need to separate them yourself, using the methods I'm going to explain. If your ex-wife decides to take that joint credit card that you've had together for ten years and go on a Target shopping spree, you don't have much recourse if you never closed that credit card.

Credit Cards

If you have joint credits cards the ideal solution is to pay them off and close the card. If this isn't an option, each party needs to open their own credit card and transfer their portion of the debt to their new card. The amount of debt each person acquires will be detailed in the decree. Then make sure that you close that joint account.

Auto Loan

If both of your names are on a car loan, but it's really your ex's car and you'll never be driving it again, you need to get your name off of that loan. This will most likely mean that the person who truly owns the car will need to refinance the loan. Go to your local bank or credit union, and apply for a new loan for that car. Or, if you can, pay it off.

Home Loan

When couples divorce, they often decide to sell the family home and each person will move to a new location. This is a great financial option, because it forces your finances to become separate. But some couples might not want to sell the house right away. If that's the case, you'll need to come to an agreement that is detailed in the decree.

Once the agreement has been reached and the divorce is final, do what it says! Don't put it off. The person staying in the house may need to pay the other party their share of the equity. It might seem like a hassle, but it's so much better to refinance the loan right away than to put it off indefinitely.

Take Maya, for instance. Six years ago, Maya and her husband divorced. She stayed in the family home so her son wouldn't have to change schools, and endure even more upheavals in his life. It worked for a while, but then the house fell into disrepair, and Maya couldn't pay for the upkeep anymore.

By a stroke of luck, the real estate market in her area appreciated like crazy. Even though her house needed some work, she was able to get a really good price for it. Here's the catch—because Maya waited so long to pay her ex his share, she had to pay him half of the current value (including the appreciation) instead of the original value of the house from six years earlier. It hurt, I promise.

This is only one example of why you need to separate your finances from each other as soon as possible. It may be a hassle, and it may cost some money, but it is so important. It will cost you much more money if you wait. Don't put this off.

Accountability Partners

Married couples who decide to tackle their finances have a distinct advantage compared to single parents—they're doing it together. They're able to discuss the budget and make decisions as a team. Assuming, of course, that they've made the decision to really work together on their financial situation. We'll assume that they have.

Single parents don't have the luxury of working on their finances with a partner. They need to, or are able to, make all budget decisions on their own. This can be both a good and a bad thing. It can be good, because as the sole custodian of your money you can do whatever you want. It can be bad for the same reason. There's no one there to say, "Let's think about that purchase for a minute; maybe we can sleep on it and see how we feel in the morning."

Bouncing important decisions off another person is always a great idea. Doing that will help keep you honest with yourself when it comes to money.

I suggest that you ask a trusted friend or family member to be your accountability partner. Be completely upfront and honest with them regarding your plan, and what you hope to accomplish. If you have questions regarding your budget, show it to them.

"Oh no!" you respond, completely shocked. Your eyes are wide with surprise. "I could never show my budget to someone else. Then they would know how much money I make!"

That's okay. Your accountability partner is allowed to know that. This is someone you trust; someone you're close to. You can share this information with them. You asked them to help because you know that they care about you. Don't be afraid to share your budget and ask them what they think.

If you're considering a large purchase, that's also a great thing to get a second opinion on. Maybe it's time for you to buy a new car, but you're not sure about the right amount of money to spend. You might not even be sure what kind of car would be the best for you. An accountability partner is a great resource to have what you have big decisions to make.

Your accountability partner is there to act as a second pair of eyes and ears.

My Partner

Name

_____

Phone Number

_____

E-Mail Address

_____

Other Contact Info

_____

Notes

_____

_____

_____

_____

_____

_____

_____

_____

_____

_____

Don't EVER Make
These Money Mistakes

The items I discuss in this chapter certainly don't apply only to single parents. Plenty of intelligent, successful individuals make these mistakes, for various reasons. Many times, it's because they're in a desperate situation and it sounds like a good idea at the time.

I have met many single parents over the years who have made these mistakes. I'll never forget when one very sweet, smart woman said to me, "I never should have done that. I wish someone had told me not to." She had cashed out her IRA (Individual Retirement Account) early, and paid a lot in taxes and penalties.

So, here you go. I'm telling you not to, and explaining why.

Cosigning

I heard a financial expert say once that people who cosign loans for others are some of the nicest people in the world. It's true—they think they're helping a friend or family member. Unfortunately, it often backfires, and the cosigner is the one who gets stuck paying off the loan.

Why would someone ask you to cosign a loan in the first place? Let's say that Jimmy goes to the bank to apply for a loan because he wants to buy a car. He found this sweet black-on-black Mustang, and he knows for a fact that the dealer up on highway 75 in McKinney has the best price in town. He HAS to have this car! He sits down to chat with the loan officer at his local credit union. He's a nice guy; Jimmy is certain he'll be able to get a loan, especially with this man helping him.

The banker reviews the application and punches some numbers into his computer.

"Jimmy," he says, with a serious look on his face, "your credit score is 675, and your monthly income doesn't seem to be high enough for you to be able to make the payment. I'm afraid you can't qualify for an auto loan."

Jimmy was crushed. He was sure this was going to work. "Isn't there anything I can do?" he asks, close to tears.

"You could get a cosigner," replies Jimmy's new best friend. "Do you think your mom or dad would be willing to do that?"

You see, the reason that Jimmy needs a cosigner, is that he does not make enough money or have a high enough credit score to qualify for the loan by himself. The bank needs a guarantee that if he does not make the payments (which seems to be very likely) someone else will.

If Jimmy does not make the payments, the cosigner is one hundred percent responsible for the loan! I've heard people say, "But I was the second signer!" or, "I don't have the car!"

These things don't matter at all to the bank. They want their money and if your name and signature are on the paper, they will come after you.

Susan was a very smart, successful single mom who I met a few years ago. She was in a fairly new relationship with a man, and she was on cloud nine. It was that dreamy beginning part of a new relationship, where he could do no wrong.

He needed to apply for a loan in order to help his mom (or so he said). He explained to Susan that his divorce had been brutal. His ex-wife had taken everything, and left him with so much debt. And, he rarely saw his children because of her. Susan's heart broke for him. She really wanted to help him.

Because of his crappy finances he needed a cosigner in order to get this loan that would help his mother buy medication that was absolutely necessary to keep her alive.

"Please, Susan, will you help me? By the way, you look lovely tonight. Let me pour some more wine for you."

Yes, of course she cosigned a loan for him.

They were together for about two more months, before Susan's guy just quit contacting her. When she reached out to him, there was no reply. Nothing. It was as if they had never known each other.

Susan didn't know what to do. She was devastated—she really thought this man cared for her, and that they had a future. But she knew she couldn't start stalking him. If he had changed his mind about her and their relationship, she supposed she needed to accept that. It just would have been better if he had told her in person.

Several months went by, and Susan moved on. Then one day, she got a phone call from the bank. Remember that loan she cosigned for her ex-boyfriend? The one who quit calling her and wouldn't take her calls? He stopped making payments on that loan, and now they were coming to Susan for the money.

"But, I don't have any of the money. I'm just the cosigner. I haven't heard from this guy in months!" These were all the reasons she gave that explained why she wasn't responsible; at least, in her mind. The bank disagreed.

"I'm sorry, ma'am. Since you are a cosigner you are 100% responsible for this loan, in the event that the other person stops making payments."

Susan was shocked. She could not believe that she was now on the hook for this loan. If she refused to make the payments, then her credit score and financial life would be destroyed.

Like I said at the beginning of this chapter; people who cosign loans for others are some of the nicest people in the world.

Title and Payday Loans

I had spent a couple hours shopping one Saturday afternoon, and I was just pulling into my driveway when my phone rang. The caller ID showed that it was Cindy, one of the single moms in the support group that I lead.

I answered with a pleasant, "Hi Cindy, how are you?" and was greeted with tears, and a frantic woman at the other end of the line.

Cindy explained to me that in a moment of desperation she had taken out a payday loan. Now, she was actually behind on her mortgage, because the payments for that short-term, predatory loan were so incredibly high.

I'm sure you've all seen the commercials on television. They promise you a loan of $1,000 to $5,000 no matter what your credit score looks like. They act like it's super-easy. When you walk into one of the storefronts they treat you like they are your best friends in the world, and they only want to help you. Don't fall for it—they're not your friends.

But when people find themselves in a desperate situation, they tend to do impulsive things. It's so hard sometimes to think rationally when you're just not sure what to do.

How does a payday or title loan work?

Here's a definition from PaydayLoanInfo.org:

> *"Payday loans are short-term cash loans based on the borrower's personal check held for future deposit or on electronic access to the borrower's bank account. Borrowers write a personal check for the amount borrowed plus the finance charge and receive cash. In some cases, borrowers sign over electronic access to their bank accounts to receive and repay payday loans.*

Lenders hold the checks until the borrower's next payday when loans and the finance charge must be paid in one lump sum. To pay a loan, borrowers can redeem the check by paying the loan with cash, allow the check to be deposited at the bank, or just pay the finance charge to roll the loan over for another pay period. Some payday lenders also offer longer-term payday instalment loans and request authorization to electronically withdraw multiple payments from the borrower's bank account, typically due on each pay date. Payday loans range in size from $100 to $1,000, depending on state legal maximums. The average loan term is about two weeks. Loans typically cost 400% annual interest (APR) or more. The finance charge ranges from $15 to $30 to borrow $100. For two-week loans, these finance charges result in interest rates from 390 to 780% APR. Shorter term loans have even higher APRs. Rates are higher in states that do not cap the maximum cost."

Make note of the interest rates—they range from 390% to 780%! This is outrageous! It's borderline illegal, and there are states who are working hard to get rid of these criminals completely. That may prove to be difficult, but one thing that is more attainable is to limit the interest that they can charge consumers.

It is illegal to have payday and title loan shops located outside of a military base. They used to love loaning money to the military, especially the young people. They were absolutely taking advantage of our soldiers. These predators were counting on the fact that many of the personnel on the bases were pretty young. Many of them joined the military right out of high school, and didn't know much about finances.

A title loan is very similar to a payday loan. The interest rates are just as high. Instead of using your next paycheck as collateral, the crooks (I mean lenders) are using your vehicle. You may have seen the commercials that brag, "I got a title loan, and I got to keep my car!"

Of course you keep your car. You're still driving it around, but the thieves (I mean lenders) are holding onto the title. They're counting on the fact that you'll stop making payments. Then, it will be completely legal for them to repossess your vehicle.

I'll never forget the call from Cindy. She was devastated.

"Diane, I don't know what do to!" she said. "I took out a payday loan, and the payments are so high that now I'm behind on my mortgage!"

Cindy is a very successful single mom. She has a good job and she owns her own home. The reason she went to a payday loan store was that she believed she was in a desperate situation. Her car needed major repair. It was her only vehicle, and she needed it in order to go to work, drive her daughter to her activities, and do everything else that a parent needs to do!

I did my best to calm her down. I urged her to stay current on her mortgage, and don't worry about the loan sharks for now. They were charging her $700 twice a month. That was more than her mortgage payment. And, guess what? The original loan was for $2,500! They had her on the hook with the enormous interest rates and fees.

If you were to find yourself in a desperate situation where you absolutely needed some money that you didn't have, you need to do everything else, before setting foot inside a payday or title loan shop.

What are some alternatives?

- Ask your family.
- Ask your boss—many employers will loan a certain amount of money to a good employee.
- Borrow from a local bank or credit union.
- Sell stuff in your home.

Whatever the alternate solution may be, make sure you're talking to a friend about what you're going through. You don't have to go through these tough times alone. Together, you'll have a better chance of coming up with a workable solution. Don't make a hasty decision based on desperation.

Action Plan

- Make sure you have an emergency fund in place, so you don't need to visit the Payday Loan crooks.
- If you're faced with a difficult decision that would require you to spend money you don't have, it's perfectly fine to just say, "No."

Make that Paycheck Go Farther

I hear it all the time. "I don't have enough money to pay my bills." I get it. Supporting yourself and your kids on one salary is not easy. It can feel like there's never enough money. But there are ways to make that paycheck last a little longer. It takes discipline and self-control. It won't be easy. Things that are important and worthwhile are rarely easy. Doing the right thing is hard. It will involve sacrifice—you won't be able to buy something whenever you want to. You will have to plan. For me, that's not a problem. I'm a compulsive planner. But I understand that not everyone is, and this may be more difficult for some of you, depending on your personality.

Force yourself to control your money. Make yourself win. The only person who can fix the problem is you. We are all responsible for our choices. Realize that what you're doing is sacrificing for a relatively short amount of time, in order to win in the long run. You're not going to have to sacrifice forever. But it's worth it.

Budget

When you decide that it's time to start winning with money, the first thing you need to do is live on a budget. You need to make a conscious decision to make a HUGE change in your life, if you want to succeed with money. You need to stop seeing yourself as a victim. You need to quit thinking that the government will support you. Do not play that single parent card! You are NOT a victim. You don't deserve handouts.

YOU ARE IN COMPLETE CONTROL OF YOUR FINANCIAL LIFE

I apologize if that sounds harsh—I'm just trying to encourage all of you to take control of your own life, without thinking you need to depend on anyone else. You don't.

When people hear the word "budget," they immediately cringe. That word brings to mind images of living on bread and water, wearing worn-out clothing, and never doing anything fun. I'm going to convince you that "budget" is not a curse word. It is simply a way of knowing where you're spending your money. The majority of Americans today have no idea what they're spending all of their money on. It's so easy today to swipe a debit or credit card, and not keep track of expenses. Then, before you know it, you don't have any money left in your checking account, and your credit card bill is sky-high.

The first step in starting a budget is to grab a piece of paper. Or, if you prefer, start a new spreadsheet on your computer. When I was first getting used to living on a budget, it was easiest for me to just write it down on a piece of paper. If I needed to cross something out, it wasn't a problem. Then, when I became more used to the categories and the numbers were pretty accurate, I started using a budget form on my computer.

Today, there are many budgeting apps to choose from. Many of them have a free version that works fine, and a version you can pay for that includes some additional features. Some of the most popular (according to NerdWallet.com) budgeting apps include:

- You Need a Budget (YNAB)
- EveryDollar
- Mint
- Goodbudget
- Personal Capital
- PocketGuard
- Honeydue
- Fudget

I still print the budget out each month, because if something does need to be changed during the month, I like to mark it up, crossing out the numbers that don't apply and writing in the new ones. Then, I save the marked up budget sheets in my file cabinet, because I am a budget sheet hoarder. Seriously, I might need them for something, someday. I might need to see what I spent my money on the week of November 3, 2008. Or, maybe not.

It doesn't matter what kind of system you use for your budget; it only matters that it works for you. Whether it's state-of-the-art high tech, or low tech, old school, it simply needs to work for you. Just make sure that you stick to that budget.

So, grab spiral notebook or a yellow legal pad, and get ready to create your very first budget!

The first thing you need to do is determine your take-home income. This is the amount of your paycheck after taxes, insurance, retirement contributions, and any other items that are deducted from your gross pay.

- Gross—Your salary before deductions.
- Net—Your salary after deductions (taxes, insurance, etc.)

Are you paid weekly, every other week, twice each month, or monthly?

Let's take a look at the different times that you might receive a paycheck:

- Every week
- Every two weeks
- Twice each month (also known as semi-monthly), typically on the fifteenth and last day of the month)
- Once each month

Each pay frequency comes with its own special set of challenges.

- Every week—When you get a paycheck every week, you feel rich. For the most part, you're able to take care of business with each paycheck. Groceries, gas for the car, most utilities. But, when you need to take care of that rent or mortgage payment, that's when budgeting comes in. You need to make sure that you hold on to some money from one paycheck to cover those bigger expenses.
- Every two weeks—This is also known as a "bi-weekly" paycheck. You'll receive your check the same day of the week, every two weeks. Throughout the year, the dates of the checks will change, so you'll have to keep a close eye on which bills need to be paid with a specific check. There's a special perk when you're paid bi-weekly. Twice each year, you'll end up with a "magic month." During this magic month, you'll receive THREE paychecks. Woo hoo! That's because there are 26 pay periods during the year. Now, this

doesn't mean that you can blow the whole thing. Make sure you incorporate that extra check into your regular monthly budget.

- Twice a Month—This one is called "semi-monthly" and paychecks are often distributed on the 15th and the last day of each month, or maybe the 16th and the first of the month. While this pay cycle is similar to every two weeks, you'll end up receiving 24 paychecks, and not 26. Therefore, no magic month. But don't worry—you still receive the same amount of money annually.

- Every Month—This is a tricky pay cycle. You'll receive a very large check, but it won't come very often. You may be tempted to go on a bit of a shopping spree when you see how much money you have. You need to resist that impulse, and stick to the budget that you've created for the entire month.

With each of these situations, you need make sure that you are spending less than you're earning. In order to do that, it's vital that you spend your money on paper *first*, so you know exactly what you'll have left. You may discover that you need to make some adjustments along the way, and that's perfectly fine.

How often do you get paid?

☐ Once a Week

☐ Every Two Weeks

☐ Twice a Month

☐ Once a Month

☐ Self-Employed/Commission Only

Next, you will need to know the exact date that all of your household bills must be paid.

If you don't know the day of the month that your regular household bills are due (rent, electricity, gas, cable, day care, car payment, etc.) then you need to figure that out NOW!

Log into your bank's website and take a look at the transaction information. This will display the dates that your bills are paid. Or, if you still have paper bills and statements gather all of them together and note the due dates on each one. That will help you determine which bills will be paid from a particular paycheck.

It might take a little bit of time to track down all of this information, but it's a vital exercise as you're creating your budget.

First, on your handy legal pad (or the worksheet included in this book), make a list of all the bills you need to pay every month. For most people, the list will look something like this:

- Rent or mortgage
- Electricity
- Natural Gas
- Cell Phone
- Internet/Cable
- City Water/Trash/Recycling
- Streaming Services

I didn't include a landline telephone because most people are using only their cell phone. This is great, because it certainly can save you money if you don't have that additional bill to worry about each month.

You may have some additional monthly expenses, such as a gym membership. I think a gym membership is very worthwhile, as long as you're using it. If you never go, cancel it immediately. There is nothing worse than paying for something every month that you aren't using. I'm a big fan of going to the gym on a regular basis. Regular exercise is a great stress-reliever, and it helps keep you healthy. Many memberships today are very reasonably priced. There are quite a few that cost only $10 each month, which is certainly do-able. IF you use it. If you're not using it, cancel it.

If you are the Non-Custodial Parent and need to make a child support payment every month, be sure to add that to your list of bills that need to be paid.

Next, you'll need to write down the day of the month that each of these bills are due. Do you still receive paper bills in the mail? Grab the most recent bills for all of your monthly payments and write down those due dates.

There will be items that are consistent in your budget, and need to be paid every month. You know that you'll always need to pay the rent, utilities, and buy groceries. And then there will be items that are not necessarily carried over from month to month.

Does your kiddo have school pictures coming up? That might be an extra budget item for that month. You might need to include fees for band or extracurricular activities. Don't forget about the Book Fair. My kids loved being able to buy a few books when the Book Fair came to their school.

While it's very important to stick to your budget as much as possible, it's understandable that things might change a little bit from one month to the next.

It may take two or three months to get used to living on a budget. You probably won't know right off the bat how much you'll spend on groceries, entertainment, and other areas that tend to fluctuate. But don't give up! You will figure it out, and you won't regret it!

Action Plan

- Log into your bank's website or gather your paper bills to figure out when every bill is due each month. Write down the bills and the payment amount on the due date on the calendar on the next page.
- Create a written budget every month.

When Are Your Bills Due?

Let's write down when every single one of your bills are due. If you still receive paper bills in the mail, gather them all together and write down the day of the month that each of these bills are due.

If you pay for bills online, log into each merchant/provider and find the due date there.

Month of _____

Sunday	Monday	Tuesday	Wednesday	Thursday	Friday	Saturday

Sample Budget

Please note—these numbers are for illustration purposes only. I understand that your budget will probably not look like this.

JUNE 11 - $1,250		
WATER/TRASH—50	GAS—70	
STREAMING SVCS—$40		
CELL PHONE—55		
GROCERIES—150	GIVING—20	WINE—20
DINING OUT—25	GAS FOR CAR—75	HOUSEHOLD - 25
ENTERTAINMENT—25	HAIRCUTS—20	CLOTHES - 25
HOLIDAYS—25	PETS—10	BLOW—25

June 25 - $1,250 + 545 = 1,795		
Rent—600		
Electricity—125		
Gym—20		
Groceries—150	Giving—20	Wine—20
Dining Out—25	Gas for Car—75	Household - 25
Entertainment—25	Haircuts—20	Clothes - 25
Holidays—25	Pets—10	Blow—25

Date and Amount		
Envelope Categories		

Date and Amount		

Envelope Categories

Notes

_____

_____

_____

_____

_____

_____

_____

_____

_____

_____

_____

The Income Issue

I know that there are many, many single parents who are truly pinching every penny. They live and die by the written budget, and they *still* have a hard time staying afloat. In this case, we might be looking at more of an "income" problem than an "outgo" problem.

There are many potential solutions to this problem, including winning the Power Ball, or inheriting millions from your rich Uncle Henry. We're going to talk about solutions that are actually in your control and that have a chance of working.

Earning More Money in Your Full-Time Job

I know too many single moms who are well-educated with years of relevant work experience, and they are simply not making enough money. They are living paycheck-to-paycheck, just scraping by. They have nothing in savings so when an emergency hits, they need to charge it, or go into debt some other way.

When I say "enough money" I believe that anyone with a college degree and several years' work experience should not have to earn less than $50,000. Still, I see it all the time. And, I do believe that this particular issue is more common among women, than among men. For some crazy reason women tend to under-value themselves in the workplace. We are very nervous when it comes to asking for more money. We shouldn't be.

Women should never underestimate the value they bring to the workplace. You're there for a reason, and it's because you are an asset to your employer. If you feel you deserve more money, then ask for it.

So, how do you make more money?

First, think about where you'd like to work. Do you want to stay at the company where you currently work, or do you want to make a change?

If you like where you work, the first thing you can do is ask your boss for a raise. Now, don't just walk into your boss' office, demanding more money. You need to create a case for yourself. The website

Salary.com is an excellent first step. Visit this site and enter information such as your job, years of experience, and where you live. Based on this information Salary.com will tell you the low, average, and high salary ranges for your position.

You should also be ready to explain why you, personally, should be paid more. Make a list of times that you've helped other employees, and gone above and beyond your typical duties.

For example, let's say that you're on the Help Desk in your company's IT department. During the year that you've worked there you have held regular training sessions, to help the employees better understand the company's software and computer systems. These sessions have been very well received and your boss has received several complimentary e-mails about you from the attendees.

These kinds of examples are definitely raise-worthy. If you are well-prepared and confident, there is no reason to be nervous.

Or, instead of asking for a raise you may be more interested in moving into a different field or department within your company. Let's stick with our Help Desk example. It's a great place to start out, but you might be interested in moving into a Network Engineering role, or perhaps you'd like to be a Project Manager.

Again, approach your supervisor and let them know that you're interested in pursuing a different role within the company. Talk about the best way to achieve that goal. You may need to take some classes, or start some specific on-the-job training.

My point is that if you don't let people at work know what your goals are, this new position will never happen for you. It's completely appropriate to talk to your supervisor, and even other supervisors within the company, to learn about growth opportunities.

Maybe you're actually interested in moving to a new company that would provide the opportunity that you're looking for. That's fine, too. In today's workplace, it's very common for people to switch companies in order to earn more money and grow professionally.

Before you begin the search for your dream job, you must make sure that your resume is up-to-date and includes all relevant skills, education, and experience.

There are several ways to go about searching for a new job. Some methods include:

- Use your own network.
- Search for jobs online.
- Use a recruiter.

Use Your Own Network

One of the best ways to get your foot in the door of a company you're interested in working for is to approach people you already know. Let your friends know that you're in the market for a new position. Send your friends your resume. This actually can serve a great dual purpose. Your friend can pass it along if a job opening becomes available, and they can provide feedback to you, if they think your resume may need some editing.

Having someone you already know working at a company is invaluable. Most hiring managers want to interview someone who is connected to an employee. This actually makes their job much easier. Don't be afraid to reach out to people you know.

An excellent professional networking resource is LinkedIn.com. LinkedIn displays where your connections work, and you can also view the employees who work for a particular company that interests you. If you notice someone who you don't know personally, but a friend of yours does, ask that friend for an introduction.

Search for Jobs Online

There are many websites online that list available jobs in your area. The one that I use most frequently is Indeed.com. Indeed.com acts as a search engine for job postings, so it is able to display jobs that are posted all over the Internet.

If you're interested in working for a particular company, make sure you frequently visit their Career page so you can be notified of job openings.

When you find a job on any site that interests you, you should apply for it. But first, you need to make sure your resume reflects how qualified you are for that specific position.

Every time you apply for a job you will need to tweak your resume to make it specific for that particular job.

Sounds like a lot of work, doesn't it? You've already put the time and effort into updating your resume. It would be so easy to simply send that resume to all of the jobs you'd like to apply for. But if you do that, you won't stand out. Why would a potential employer choose your resume over the many others that they receive?

Employers want to see exactly why you would be the best fit for that job. Take the time to address the skills and other requirements that they are looking for every single time you apply for a job.

Use a Recruiter

I absolutely LOVE working with a recruiter when I'm searching for my next great job. If you work with a recruiter or temp agency, they are just as motivated as you are to find your next employer, because they're going to be paid when you're hired.

Practically every industry is represented by a form of staffing agency. Whether you're looking for a job in IT, the medical field, or even as a writer, you can find an agency who wants to help you get a new job.

Recruiters work with companies who need to hire new employees for various positions. So they will know exactly what a company's needs are, and what kind of skills it will take to fill those needs. Recruiters will never put a candidate in an interview position if they don't think they would be a good fit. So if a recruiter is able to schedule an interview for you, it's because they already think you have the skills and experience required for that job. Then it's up to you to knock 'em dead at the interview!

Another great advantage of working with a recruiter is that they can help you polish your resume. They'll give you advice on wording and formatting, and also catch any errors you might have missed.

The best way to find a recruiter or staffing agency is to start searching on the Internet. You will be surprised at how many people really want to help you find a job.

Action Plan

- Update your resume.
- Customize your resume for every single job you apply for.
- If you want to stay with your current company, talk to your supervisor.
- If you'd like to search for a new job, reach out to your network and recruiters.
- Use this planner that begins on the next page to form a plan to succeed in your chosen career.

Whether you're looking for work, working in a job you don't love, or even lucky enough to be doing your dream job, it never hurts to evaluate where you are and how you can grow. Kudos on you for taking the initiative! Use the space below to work on laying out your career objectives.

CAREER OBJECTIVES

What do you hope this workbook can help you with?

_____
_____
_____
_____
_____
_____
_____

Where do you see yourself in 5 years?

_____
_____
_____
_____
_____
_____
_____

How committed are you to changing your circumstances?

1 Uncommitted　　⊛　⊛　⊛　⊛　⊛　⊛　⊛　⊛　⊛　　10 Very Committed

What is at stake if you do not achieve your career goals?

_____
_____
_____
_____
_____
_____

Everyone has something that they would love to be doing as a career. However, not all of us are actually doing that job. That doesn't mean you are stuck there. Use the space below to figure out where you are and create a strategy that can bring you to that path to doing what you love.

WHAT'S YOUR DREAM JOB?

What is your dream job?

_____
_____
_____
_____

Are you doing that?

     Yes   No

If not, why? What has kept you from it?

_____
_____
_____
_____

How can you overcome these obstacles?

_____
_____
_____
_____

If you are in your dream career, is there any room for you to grow?

     Yes   No

If yes, how?

_____
_____
_____
_____

MOVING UP

If you're in a job that you want to stay in, chances are that there are a lot of opportunities around you to grow within that career. Allowing yourself to go after promotions increases your experience, keeps you from stagnating, and can also give you more money to put away for your retirement. On the next page, list the positions you believe you qualify for and/or want to do.

PROMOTION POSSIBILITY

○ Job Title: _____

_____

_____

○ What qualifies you to take this position?

_____

_____

_____

_____

_____

_____

_____

_____

_____

○ Is this a lateral or upward move?

⦿ Lateral   ⦿ Upward

○ Will this take you closer or further to your goal?

⦿ Further   ⦿ Neither   ⦿ Closer

○ How much would you like to have this position?

1 Not Much   ⦿ ⦿ ⦿ ⦿ ⦿ ⦿ ⦿ ⦿ ⦿ ⦿   10 Very Much

○ How likely will you get this position?

1 Unlikely   ⦿ ⦿ ⦿ ⦿ ⦿ ⦿ ⦿ ⦿ ⦿ ⦿   10 Likely

○ What steps should you take next to go after this position?

_____

_____

_____

_____

_____

_____

_____

_____

PROMOTION POSSIBILITY

○ Job Title: _____

_____

_____

○ What qualifies you to take this position?

_____

_____

_____

_____

_____

_____

_____

_____

_____

_____

○ Is this a lateral or upward move?

⦾ Lateral ⦾ Upward

○ Will this take you closer or further to your goal?

⦾ Further ⦾ Neither ⦾ Closer

○ How much would you like to have this position?

I Not Much ⦾ ⦾ ⦾ ⦾ ⦾ ⦾ ⦾ ⦾ ⦾ ⦾ 10 Very Much

○ How likely will you get this position?

I Unlikely ⦾ ⦾ ⦾ ⦾ ⦾ ⦾ ⦾ ⦾ ⦾ ⦾ 10 Likely

○ What steps should you take next to go after this position?

_____

_____

_____

_____

_____

_____

_____

PROMOTION POSSIBILITY

Job Title: _____

_____

_____

What qualifies you to take this position?

_____

_____

_____

_____

_____

_____

_____

_____

Is this a lateral or upward move?

○ Lateral   ○ Upward

Will this take you closer or further to your goal?

○ Further   ○ Neither   ○ Closer

How much would you like to have this position?

1 Not Much ○ ○ ○ ○ ○ ○ ○ ○ ○ ○ 10 Very Much

How likely will you get this position?

1 Unlikely ○ ○ ○ ○ ○ ○ ○ ○ ○ ○ 10 Likely

What steps should you take next to go after this position?

_____

_____

_____

_____

_____

_____

_____

Now that you know which position(s) you have an interest in, it's time to figure out what steps you need to take to get there. Write down the ways you can start working towards the position you're after, and how you can improve in the position you're in now to show your potential to move upward.

PROMOTION PROGRESS

Position: _____

What skills do you already possess for this position?

_____
_____
_____

What skills do you need to acquire to get this position?

_____
_____
_____

Other factors

_____
_____

Position: _____

What skills do you already possess for this position?

_____
_____
_____

What skills do you need to acquire to get this position?

_____
_____
_____

Other factors

_____
_____

Notes: _____
_____
_____
_____

PROMOTION PROGRESS

○ Position: _____

○ What skills do you already possess for this position?
_____
_____

○ What skills do you need to acquire to get this position?
_____
_____

○ Other factors
_____
_____

○ Position: _____

○ What skills do you already possess for this position?
_____
_____

○ What skills do you need to acquire to get this position?
_____
_____

○ Other factors
_____
_____

MOVING ON

If getting a promotion or new position wherever you are now isn't what you want, and you don't want to stay, it could be time to move on from your current job. However, it's not smart to just quit without knowing where you're going to go next. Ideally, you should have a new job lined up before leaving.

The first step to doing this is figuring out what you want to do next, and where the best place to do that is. Use the next page to research some new opportunities that you'd be interested in moving on to, whether you have the qualifications already or want to start fresh.

POTENTIAL PLACE TO MOVE ON TO

○ Company / Industry:

_____

_____

_____

○ Job Title: _____

○ Why this company?

_____

○ What skills are they looking for?

_____

_____

_____

○ What qualifies you to take this position?

_____

_____

_____

○ What skills do you need to have to get this position?

_____

_____

_____

○ How big a gap is it between your qualifications and what the company is looking for?

_____

_____

_____

○ Can you realistically bridge the gap right now?

○ Yes   ○ Possibly   ○ No

○ How big a gap is it between your qualifications and what the company is looking for?

_____

_____

_____

_____

POTENTIAL PLACE TO MOVE ON TO

Company / Industry:

_____

_____

_____

Job Title: _____

Why this company?

_____

What skills are they looking for?

_____

_____

_____

What qualifies you to take this position?

_____

_____

_____

What skills do you need to have to get this position?

_____

_____

_____

How big a gap is it between your qualifications and what the company is looking for?

_____

_____

_____

Can you realistically bridge the gap right now?

    ○ Yes   ○ Possibly   ○ No

How big a gap is it between your qualifications and what the company is looking for?

_____

_____

_____

_____

POTENTIAL PLACE TO MOVE ON TO

Company / Industry:

_____

_____

Job Title: _____

Why this company?

_____

What skills are they looking for?

_____

_____

What qualifies you to take this position?

_____

_____

What skills do you need to have to get this position?

_____

_____

How big a gap is it between your qualifications and what the company is looking for?

_____

_____

Can you realistically bridge the gap right now?

○ Yes   ○ Possibly   ○ No

How big a gap is it between your qualifications and what the company is looking for?

_____

_____

_____

EXITING GRACEFULLY

Depending on how long you have been in your current position, and what responsibilities you have, leaving might not be as simple as 2 weeks notice. You may need to train a replacement, work on creating some best practice materials, and/or more. The key is not leaving with bad blood, or any kind of ill will. It's always better to leave a job with as much dignity and politeness as possible, so that you can use the experience and references to help you build the future career you want. Below, list the final duties you can work on to prepare your current team for your departure, and set them up for success.

○ Task 1: Write notice letter

○ Task 2: Create a document with your list of daily duties and average time to complete

○ Task 3: Finish any open tasks/tie up loose ends

○ Task 4: Make a training/orientation folder for your replacement

○ Task 5: Do prep work for incoming projects

○ Task 6: Request letters of recommendation from supervisors

○ Task 7: Train/recommend replacement

○ Task 8: _____

○ Task 9: _____

○ Task 10: _____

○ Task 11: _____

○ Task 12: _____

EXITING GRACEFULLY

○ Task 1: _____

_____

_____

○ Task 2: _____

_____

○ Task 3: _____

○ Task 4: _____

○ Task 5: _____

○ Task 6: _____

○ Task 7: _____

○ Task 8: _____

○ Task 9: _____

○ Task 10: _____

○ Task 11: _____

○ Task 12: _____

○ Task 13: _____

○ Task 14: _____

In a previous exercise, you created a list of potential jobs that you could see yourself moving on to. Now, it's time to expand on that and really evaluate what's going to be the best fit for you and your skills. Depending on whether or not you've already been doing the job(s) that interest you, you may need to rework and get creative about how your skills can be utilized for a new job. Use the space below to evaluate how your skills fit into the jobs you want.

APPLY YOUR EXISTING SKILLS

Company: _____

Title: _____

How can you apply your skills?

_____

_____

_____

_____

_____

_____

_____

_____

Company: _____

Title: _____

How can you apply your skills?

_____

_____

_____

_____

_____

_____

_____

_____

APPLY YOUR EXISTING SKILLS

○ Company: _____
_____
○ Title: _____
○ _____
○ How can you apply your skills?
_____
_____
_____
_____
_____

○ Company: _____
○ Title: _____
○ How can you apply your skills?
_____
_____
_____
_____
_____

○ Company: _____
○ Title: _____
○ How can you apply your skills?
_____
_____
_____
_____
_____
_____

UPDATE YOUR RESUME

Now that you have a solid grasp of exactly what you want to do, and how your current skills can be utilized, it's time to update that resume! Your resume is basically the first impression you're going to make on your potential employer, so it's important to make sure that it is well formatted, updated, clear, relevant, and concise.

The basic things you need to have on your resume are: name, contact info, experience/work history, education, certifications, references, and any possible achievements or awards you've received for your work. Depending on what kind of job you're applying for, you may need to provide examples of your work, or other documents. Use the space below to check off all the elements you need for your resume, and make sure it's ready to send to potential employers.

- ○ Name
- ○ Email
- ○ Phone Number
- ○ Work History
- ○ Relevant Experience
- ○ References
- ○ Education
- ○ Certifications
- ○ Awards
- ○ Formatting
- ○ Spelling/Grammar Check
- ○ _____
- ○ _____
- ○ _____
- ○ _____
- ○ _____
- ○ _____
- ○ _____
- ○ _____

NETWORKING

Now that you have your professional ducks in a row, it's time to focus on the next thing that's going to get you the job you want. Networking is an invaluable skill for getting the jobs you want, keeping them, and moving up within them. When it comes to networking for jobs, it's important to do your research and understand the language, culture, objectives, and overall "brand" of the company/companies you'll be working with. Use the space below to get a feel for the field you're looking to get into, and then find places online or in person to connect with others who are in it...

○ Field of Interest: _____

_____

_____

_____

_____

○ Possible Companies: _____

_____

_____

_____

○ Objectives of Field: _____

_____

_____

_____

○ Language/Culture of Field: _____

_____

_____

_____

_____

○ Places to Network with Others in Field: _____

_____

_____

_____

_____

SOCIAL MEDIA AUDIT

These days, what's on your social media can make or break your career in some cases. Of course, social media is ideally a place where you can be yourself and express your thoughts about things. However, this isn't always conducive to certain professions. Many careers require that even personal online accounts represent a professional and "on brand" projection.

For many of us, an easy way around this is to simply make all socials private and not become friends with any coworkers. However, it never hurts to do a quick audit of your pages and make sure everything's on the up and up. This is especially true if your accounts are several years old, since things you might have posted years ago before you started your career might not reflect who you are now. Use the space below to check off each of your personal social accounts as you clean them up and make them more career-friendly.

○ Facebook	◎ Cleanup	◎ Update
○ Instagram	◎ Cleanup	◎ Update
○ TikTok	◎ Cleanup	◎ Update
○ Twitter	◎ Cleanup	◎ Update
○ YouTube	◎ Cleanup	◎ Update
○ LinkedIn	◎ Cleanup	◎ Update

○ _____	◎ Cleanup	◎ Update
○ _____	◎ Cleanup	◎ Update
○ _____	◎ Cleanup	◎ Update
○ _____	◎ Cleanup	◎ Update
○ _____	◎ Cleanup	◎ Update
○ _____	◎ Cleanup	◎ Update
○ _____	◎ Cleanup	◎ Update
○ _____	◎ Cleanup	◎ Update
○ _____	◎ Cleanup	◎ Update
○ _____	◎ Cleanup	◎ Update
○ _____	◎ Cleanup	◎ Update

There is always room for growth and improvement, no matter how long you've been pursuing your career. However, it's important to have a plan that you can follow to achieve that growth. When you show initiative to improve, a good employer will notice, and not only help you, but reward you as well.

GROWING YOUR SKILLS

What are your greatest challenges/weaknesses in your field?

_____

_____

_____

_____

How can you strengthen them?

_____

_____

_____

_____

_____

What classes or courses can you find to help you improve your skills overall?

_____

_____

_____

_____

_____

Is there anyone you know with more experience who you can ask to mentor you?

_____

_____

_____

_____

_____

SHIFTING YOUR SKILLS

Now, growing your skills is all well and good. However, if you're looking to shift your career direction, it's a good idea to figure out how to apply the skills you have built to your new field. Chances are, there are several ways you can pivot what you already know into a leg up for your new venture. A key way to achieve this is to be creative, and try as much as possible to generalize your skills, so you can get them to fit into your new role(s).

For example, if you've been a receptionist, you can say that you have built great organizational, interpersonal, and time management skills that can be applied to just about any job. On the next page, create a list of your skills and how you can apply them to the new direction you're working towards.

SKILL SHIFTING

○ Skill: _____

_____

_____

○ How to shift it to a new field:

_____

_____

_____

_____

_____

_____

○ Skill: _____

○ How to shift it to a new field:

_____

_____

_____

_____

_____

_____

_____

○ Skill: _____

○ How to shift it to a new field:

_____

_____

_____

_____

_____

_____

_____

**SKILL
SHIFTING**

Skill: _____
_____
_____

How to shift it to a new field:

_____
_____
_____
_____
_____
_____

Skill: _____

How to shift it to a new field:

_____
_____
_____
_____
_____
_____

Skill: _____

How to shift it to a new field:

_____
_____
_____
_____
_____
_____

INTERVIEWING WELL

Now that you have laid the groundwork with your career goals, resume, networking, and skills, it's time to prepare for the interview process. This can seem like a daunting task, and many people get very anxious before interviews. However, with a little preparation, you can ace it. Stay calm, and have just a few answers ready, you can use that as a platform to work off of and nail your interview every time. On the next page, research common interview questions in your field, and figure out how you can answer them.

INTERVIEW PREP

Possible interview question:

_____

_____

_____

_____

My answer:

_____

_____

_____

_____

Possible interview question:

_____

_____

_____

My answer:

_____

_____

_____

_____

Possible interview question:

_____

_____

_____

My answer:

_____

_____

_____

_____

INTERVIEW PREP

○ Possible interview question:

_____

_____

_____

_____

○ My answer:

_____

_____

_____

_____

_____

○ Possible interview question:

_____

_____

_____

○ My answer:

_____

_____

_____

_____

○ Possible interview question:

_____

_____

_____

○ My answer:

_____

_____

_____

_____

APPLICATION TRACKER

Company: _____

_____

_____

Job title: _____

_____

Application date: _____ / _____ / _____

○ Called for interview   Interview date: _____ / _____ / _____

Interview review notes

_____

_____

_____

_____

_____

Result: ○ Hired   ○ Turned Down

Company: _____

Job title: _____

_____

Application date: _____ / _____ / _____

○ Called for interview   Interview date: _____ / _____ / _____

Interview review notes

_____

_____

_____

_____

_____

Result: ○ Hired   ○ Turned Down

APPLICATION TRACKER

○ Company: _____

_____

_____

○ Job title: _____

_____

○ Application date: _____ / _____ / _____

○ Called for interview   Interview date: _____ / _____ / _____

○ Interview review notes

_____

_____

_____

_____

_____

○ Result: ○ Hired   ○ Turned Down

○ Company: _____
○ Job title: _____

_____

○ Application date: _____ / _____ / _____

○ Called for interview   Interview date: _____ / _____ / _____

○ Interview review notes

_____

_____

_____

_____

_____

○ Result: ○ Hired   ○ Turned Down

Hopefully, this exercise has proven valuable to you, opened your eyes to the many opportunities you have, and made apparent what your strengths and weaknesses are. Now, let's look to the future and make a plan on how to move forward.

LOOKING AHEAD

Where do you see yourself a year from now?

_____
_____
_____
_____

What do you need to do to get there?

_____
_____
_____
_____

Where do you see yourself 3 years from now?

_____
_____
_____

What needs to happen for you to get there?

_____
_____
_____

Where do you hope to be 5 years from now?

_____
_____
_____

What needs to happen for you to get there?

_____
_____
_____
_____

NOTES

Starting a Side Business

I love supporting single parents who really want to win. They don't approach life thinking they're a victim, or that they are entitled to hand-outs because they're in a difficult situation. These parents know they can be successful, and they want to learn how.

I recently met Bobbie, a single mom with two daughters. She had a job she enjoyed. The pay was okay and she had good health insurance, but it wasn't her passion. I think that's true for many of us, and there's nothing wrong with that. We go to work and we earn a paycheck that allows us to pay our rent and put food on the table. The people we work with are nice. We earn vacation time, and sick time. We're able to take time off, or work from home, when the kiddoes need us. But the industry in which we work is not necessarily something that really excites us. And that's okay.

You're doing the right thing by supporting your family. You can't just quit your job, and do whatever you feel like. That's not what adults do. What you *can* do is take your passion and turn it into a side business that could, one day, become a full-time career for you.

Bobbie worked in a doctor's office as the Office Manager. It was a good job, and she was very grateful for it. But she had the dream of starting her own small translation company. Bobbie was a native Spanish speaker, and she knew that there was a large market for translation where she lived. She started to do a little research on the Internet, and she saw there were opportunities in various industries. Translators were need in courthouses, hospitals, schools, and law offices.

So far, this idea was just that; a dream, an inkling. Bobbie wasn't sure how to turn her dream into a reality. She reached out to me, and asked what she needed to do. What are the steps you need to take if you want to turn an idea or a hobby into a business?

I was thrilled that she came to me with that question. I love the idea of taking something that you love, something that you do for fun, and turning it into a business. Now, when I say the word "business" it doesn't mean that you're going to start earning thousands of dollars immediately. It's all right to start slowly. You'll probably want to start out by looking at your business as a hobby, and realizing that it will take some time before you start earning money.

Do NOT quit your day job, thinking that you'll be able to support yourself with your new, glorious business right away. I've known people who have done this, and it did <u>not</u> go well. It's great to be excited and hopeful that you're going to be a small business owner, but you still need to pay the rent and put food on the table.

Have you heard the term, "You need to spend money to make money?" This is a myth. I used to know someone who spent a ton of money that he didn't have on website development, a business advisor, and a professional organizer. Obviously, this will just deplete your savings or send you into debt.

The resources available on the Internet make it very easy and affordable to set up a website and create a web presence.

So, what do you need to get started?

Step One

First, you need to register a domain name. Your domain name reflects the name of your business, and it is the name of your website, such as, www.MotinaBooks.com. In my example, **MotinaBooks.com** is the domain name. Choosing a domain name is an important part of choosing a name for your business. It's becoming a little bit difficult to find available domain names today, so you may need to be creative.

There are many companies that allow you to search for and register domain names. One of the most popular, and the one that I use most frequently, is www.GoDaddy.com. In the search field on their home page, enter a domain name that you would like to use, and click the "Search" button to see if it's available. Make sure that you include the "extension," such as .com, .org, or .net.

If you are searching for a domain name for your business, it's best to find a domain name that has a dot-com extension. Typically, a dot-com is used for a business, and a dot-org domain name is used for a non-profit organization.

It is becoming more difficult to find a good dot-com domain name that fits with your business name; so many of them have already been purchased. Because of this issue additional domain extensions are being made available. They're really pretty fun—you can buy a domain name that has dot-author, dot-horse, dot-dog, and even dot-wtf.

The cost to register a domain name is very reasonable. It's between $10 and $20 for one year. A whole year! It's very inexpensive. The new extensions are a bit more pricey, but still very reasonable. Have fun searching!

Step Two

So, now that you have a domain name, you can't just let it sit around, doing nothing. Put it to work!

It's time to create a website. Don't let that intimidate you; do-it-yourself website services are all over the place, and they are also very reasonably priced. GoDaddy offers several options, including a free option. Personally, I think it's worth $10 to $20 a month to have an attractive, ad-free website. I'm not going to cover all of the website options in this chapter. It's very easy to find affordable solutions.

WordPress is a powerful, yet easy-to-learn, tool that you can use to build your own site. Some other options that include gorgeous graphics are Wix and SquareSpace. You absolutely don't need to be a technical genius to build a beautiful website for your small business.

Step Three

Once you have a domain name and a website, it's time to get the word out. Order business cards, attend networking groups, send press releases, create a presence for your business on multiple social networking sites. Given the power that the Internet provides to business owners, getting the word out about your new venture should not take much money at all. You will most likely need to invest more *time* into marketing your business than money.

A great way to let people know about your business, and make them want to work with you, is to provide valuable information for free. Are you a baker that sells cupcakes and sourdough bread? Offer some recipes online that customers can try at home. Do you make and sell custom jewelry? Show some step-by-step instructions for making a beautiful necklace or bracelet. Of course, you don't have to give away any of your secrets. This information will give you and your company credibility. People will want to buy your products if they don't feel like you're only trying to sell them something.

This principle can also be applied if you already are a business owner, but would like to grow. Nicole is a single mom who has been self-employed as a manicurist for several years. She told me that she makes good money when she has enough customers, but she wasn't as busy as she'd like to be.

She handed me her business card, and asked for advice. The first thing I noticed on the pretty card with the light green background was that a website or e-mail address were not listed. Nicole expected clients to reach out to her by texting or calling. This is fine for existing clients, but how would new ones find her?

Nicole is lucky because both women and men love to get their nails done. There's nothing better than sitting in that massage chair, soaking your tootsies in warm water, while someone massages your calves and feet, then makes your toenails look gorgeous. Heaven!

I believe Nicole could easily expand her business by completing a few easy tasks that don't cost much money at all. Let's take a look:

- Get a domain name and website, using the method I explained earlier. All businesses today MUST have an Internet presence, and a website is a very important part of that.
- Clearly describe services and pricing on the website.
- Come up with some special "packages" for weddings, proms, mother/daughter dates, etc.
- Offer some services that are specific for men. This would be a unique offering, and will help her business stand out from the competition.
- Create a business page on Facebook, Instagram, Twitter, etc. And post frequently.
- Create a loyal customer "punch card" —for every ten pedicures, you get one free.3Offer a special first-time, introductory rate.

Nicole has another advantage, in that she makes her own sugar and salt scrubs that she uses when doing pedicures. She could easily create a "Products" page on her website and sell that online. People love down-to-earth products like homemade scrubs that use natural ingredients.

Now, I do realize that these suggestions are specific to one type of business. But, I hope you get the idea that it can be so much fun to be creative, and brainstorm how you can make your business grow, whether it's a small side business to help increase your income, or your full-time career.

Action Plan

- Start turning your passion into profits.

The Outgo Issue

It is possible that you're not unhappy with your salary. You may feel that you earn enough money to pay your bills, and you should be able to be saving for emergencies and retirement. So, why isn't that happening?

We've already discussed how a written budget can help you control how much is coming in, and how much is going out. It truly contributes to a feeling of freedom, and reduces the stress that can accompany not having any idea what's going on with your money. I remember the many sleepless nights that I spent, wondering how I would make the next mortgage payment.

In this section we'll discuss additional tools that will help you take control of the money that is leaving your checking account.

Envelopes

I am madly in love with the envelope system. I will continue to use this system until the day that I die. If I become a multi-millionaire tomorrow, I will still use envelopes.

In this day and age of swiping a card whenever you want to pay for something, it has become pretty unusual to pay for purchases with cash. Most people don't carry that much cash around anymore. Not when it's so easy to swipe a card, or even use your smart phone to buy things.

But there is magic when you pay for something with cash. It has a different feeling than swiping a card. You see the bills, and you feel them against your skin. I know that you'll hear the cashier tell you that an item costs a certain amount, and that's the amount that will be taken from your checking account (if you're paying with a debit card). But the feeling that you will have by paying with the actual bills that you feel in your hand is still a different than simply swiping a card. It becomes personal.

According to a Forbes article from July, 2018 multiple studies have shown that people spend more money when swiping than when they use cash. It's just too easy.

So what exactly is the envelope system? It's really very simple. Just get a stack of plain white envelopes. On each envelope you will write the name of a category. You can start out by just having a few categories that are very important to you. For example, Groceries is an important envelope category. I remember there was a time that I would go to the grocery store practically every day, without really knowing how much I was spending each time. It was so easy just to swipe a debit card and buy what I wanted; not necessarily what I needed.

But having an envelope that contained cash specifically for me to use to buy groceries for my family really helped me get a handle on how much I was spending at the store. It also helped me realize that there's a big difference between the things I want and the things I need.

It might take you a little while to realize exactly how much money you need to put into your Grocery envelope. When I first started using this system I decided to put a certain amount of money into the envelope. My daughter and I went to the store and as I put an item in the cart she would write down what the item was and how much it cost. She was keeping a running tally for me. At the end of our shopping trip I realized that we were over budget. So together my daughter and I looked at the items in the cart and we decided that we didn't really need everything we had grabbed. We put some of those items back until we met our grocery budget. We knew that we could purchase those items the next time we went shopping.

So, what are important envelope categories? We already discussed groceries, which is a big one. Number two in importance is Dining Out. You determine how much money is added to this envelope each time you are paid, and if there isn't any money in there, then you're not going to go out to eat. Entertainment is another great category. If your kids want to go to the movies, they'll need to check the Entertainment envelope first and see if there's enough money. Clothing is also a great category because children do tend to grow out of their clothes quickly.

One of my favorites is the Haircut envelope. I had three kids living in my house who frequently decided they needed a haircut all at the same time. This expense can quickly add up. As long as there was money in the envelope, they could get their haircuts. Now this envelope is a little different than the groceries envelope. When you're using the money in the groceries envelope, you will most likely empty it before your next payday. However, with envelopes such as Haircuts, the money in that envelope will accumulate until you need to use it. This is what is known as "a sinking fund." You are saving money over time to be used for a specific purpose.

My favorite sinking fund envelope, of course, is my Christmas envelope. If you don't celebrate the Christmas holiday, but still celebrate the season, this will still work for you. Write any name that works for you on the envelope.

Some of you may remember when banks offered a Christmas club. The envelope works the same way. You determine the amount of money that you'd like to contribute to your Christmas envelope every time you get paid. At the end of the year this is the money that you'll use to buy gifts for your friends and family.

In order to determine the right amount to save in that envelope, you need to first figure out how much money you want to spend on gifts for each person. This certainly includes your kids. You don't need to spend hundreds of dollars on Christmas gifts for each child.

I have found that having a Christmas envelope really helps cut down on the stress and chaos that the holiday season can bring. If you're not worrying about how to pay for Christmas gifts you really have the opportunity to enjoy the season with your family and friends. You can make sure that you are thinking more about how to make memories with your kiddoes instead of how you're going to buy the hottest toy.

If you have kids who no longer believe in Santa, don't be afraid to tell them how much money you will be spending on their gifts. They should be part of the budgeting process and they should know how much money is being allocated for the Christmas envelope every time you are paid. If they are older they might prefer to simply have the cash. This way they could combine it with other cash gifts, or cash that they are earning on their own, to buy a more expensive, special item.

My Christmas gift amount for each of my three children was $100. When my youngest son was ten he was obsessed with Legos; especially Star Wars Legos. Any time he had extra money he wanted to buy more. He even found his older brother's unassembled Millennium Falcon. There were several hundred pieces in a box with no instructions. But this did not discourage him, We were able to find the assembly instructions online. He spent hours building that spaceship. And he did a great job!

Several weeks before Christmas that year I helped him write a letter to family members who lived in other states. He explained how he loved working on Legos, and that he would really love to build the Death Star. Unfortunately, the Death Star cost well over $200, so it was obviously beyond his $100 gift budget. In the letter, we included a picture of him surrounded by all of his Lego creations. We explained that instead of tangible gifts he would prefer cash gifts so he could purchase the Death Star and build it. This worked very well. He was able to add enough money from other gifts to the $100 from the Christmas envelope to make the purchase. This exercise really helped him understand the value of that item.

Another sinking fund envelope that goes along with the Christmas envelope is one that I call Giving. This is a great envelope if you need to buy gifts for a birthday party that your child is attending, a gift for a relative, a donation to the lady at work who was having a baby shower, or any other type of gift that you can think of. There were times when it seemed my kids were going to a birthday party every week! The Giving envelope was a life saver.

How about car maintenance? If you have a car maintenance envelope you can use it for regular oil changes and smaller repairs that always come up. Larger, more expensive, repairs might need to come out of your emergency fund.

If you have pets, a Pet Needs envelope is very important. This can help pay for vet bills and also food and regular medication, like heartworm and flea prevention. If you have babies a Diaper or Formula envelope could be very useful. Now, I'm not saying that if the envelope is empty and you don't have diapers, you can't buy them. But if you have a separate category for diapers you will be able to budget more effectively. It's easier to budget if these items are not coming out of your grocery envelope.

You can create envelopes for as few or as many categories as you think are necessary. When I first started using envelopes I may have gone a little overboard with my categories, and I created a few too many. But they helped me realize how much control I now had over my finances.

An enormous advantage of using the envelope system is that it will help your children learn how much different items cost. When you shop for groceries together or go out for dinner, they will see the actual dollar bills that come out of the envelope that is dedicated especially for that purpose.

Every time you are paid whether it is once a week, every two weeks, twice a month, or once a month, you will go to the bank and withdraw a certain amount of cash to stuff within certain envelopes. I know, I know. It sounds like a real pain in the neck. I have had so many people tell me how inconvenient that is. They don't have time to go to the bank and get cash. They don't like having to plan ahead.

Once when I was presenting at a financial seminar a gentleman asked me, "So I have to know if I'm going to go out to dinner that night and bring an envelope with me?" The answer to that question, of course, is, "Yes."

Planning just a little bit really isn't that difficult. The same gentleman asked me, "What do I do with all of the coins that I receive as change?" I had a good response to this question. Who doesn't enjoy filling up a jar with coins in anticipation of using those coins for a fun purchase? They can really add up.

While you are in the process of getting your finances on track, the envelope system is an excellent tool. As time goes on and you are really starting to win with your money you may choose to continue using the envelopes like I did, or you may choose to cut back on them a bit. But this is the best system for understanding how much things cost and where you are spending your money.

Now, you might be thinking that a paper envelope system is old-school and low-tech. In this day and age when everything you do is online, or performed by an app, why do you need paper envelopes? If you prefer to use an application to manage your digital envelopes, that is definitely possible.

There are many budgeting apps available that provide this digital envelope system. You create categories within the app, then enter a spending limit within each category. The catch is that any time you make a purchase you need to remember to enter that purchase into the category. Otherwise, your checking account and your digital envelopes might get a bit out of whack.

For example, if you go out for dinner and spend $25 using your debit card, you know that money will come directly out of your checking account. But, it won't automatically be deducted from your Dining category. You need to do that, so know how much money is available in that particular category.

Also, if you use envelopes for categories like **Holidays, Giving, Household**, and **Haircuts**, your checking account is going to grow. You won't use that money every paycheck; it's meant to grow, until the time that you need to spend some of it. You may think you have more money in that account than you actually do—that's because you have money allocated in categories that are supposed to grow.

So if you log into your bank or credit union to take a look at your checking account, so you can see what came in and what went out, it may look like you have more money than you actually do. Your digital envelopes will probably only appear in your budgeting app, and not in the online view of your bank account.

That's why I still like using envelopes that I can hold in my hand. I can see exactly how much money is in each one. I love seeing how "fat" that Christmas envelope is in October. I also loved when one of my kids would ask for Chick-Fil-A and I'd have to say, "No, honey, the **Dining** envelope is empty. But we can fill it up on Friday, when I get paid."

That's such a great lesson. It helps our kids learn that money comes from working, and that we only buy something when we have the money available.

I'll use those old-fashioned paper envelopes for the rest of my life. Does it mean that I need to plan my day a little more carefully, so I put the right envelope in my purse? Sure, but that's okay.

I have a small safe on the floor in my closet, and that's where my envelopes live. For me, that's what makes sense. I know exactly how much money is in my checking account, and in my envelopes.

You need choose the method that works best for you!

Action Plan

- Label envelopes with the names of spending categories.
- Stuff the envelopes every time you are paid.

Examples of Envelope Categories

GROCERIES	EATING OUT	HOLIDAYS
CLOTHING	CAR	HOUSEHOLD
HAIRCUTS	ENTERTAIN	GIFTS
SCHOOL ACTIVITIES	BIRTHDAYS	PETS

YOUR Envelope Categories

You can have as few or as many envelope categories as you think are necessary. I tend to err on the side of more is better. It makes me feel more in control of my money!

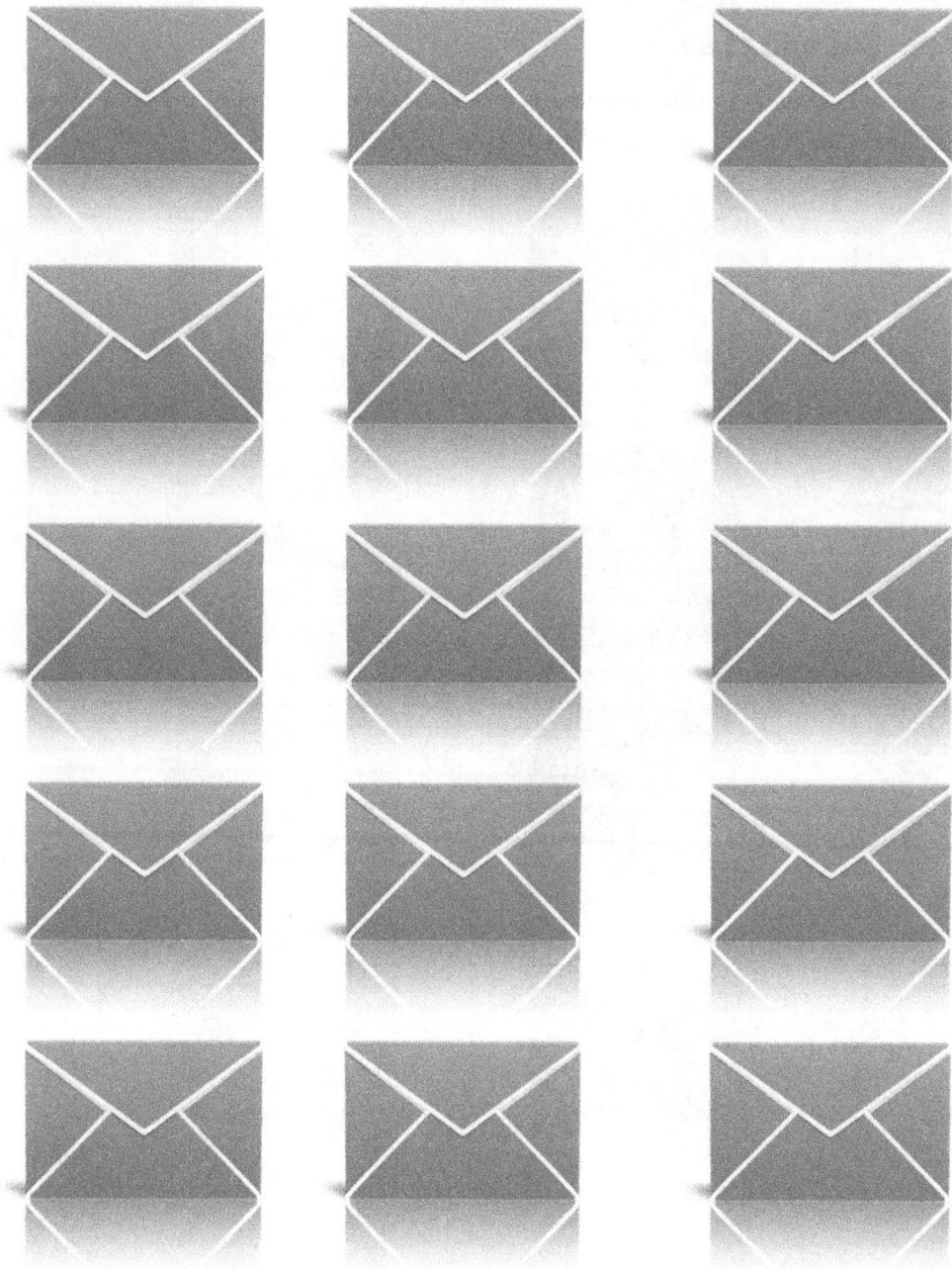

SHOW YOUR PAYCHECK WHO'S BOSS!

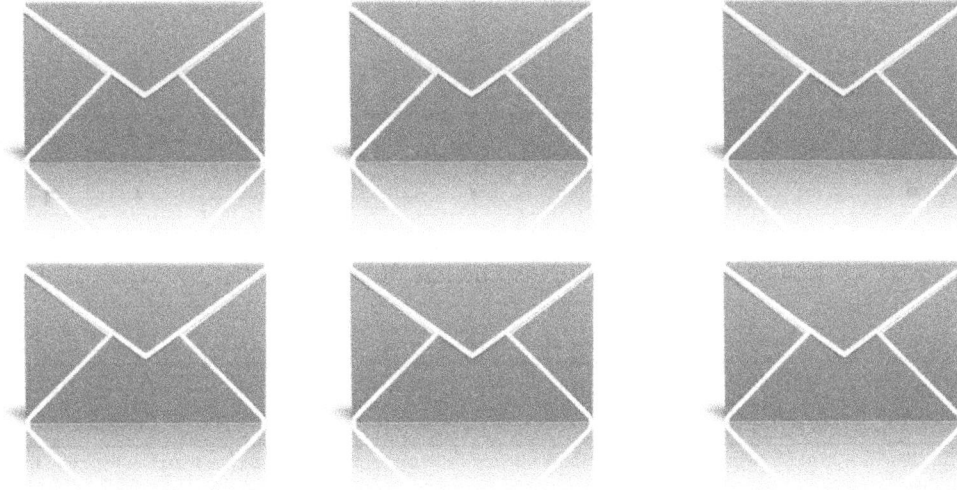

Notes

_____

_____

_____

_____

_____

_____

_____

_____

_____

_____

Cutting Back

Delia and her daughter have a very fun tradition, once every month. They go on a mother-daughter-date to their favorite salon, and get a mani-pedi. Delia told me that they look forward to this day so much. No matter what happened during the month, they make sure that nothing else is scheduled on that special day.

The two of them spend about 90 minutes having their legs and arms massaged with hot stones and fragrant lotions. They chat about school, clothes, and boys. It's a lovely outing for both of them, and their fingernails and toe nails always look fabulous. The only downside is the $200 bill that the salon charges.

Delia usually pulls out her credit card and charges the mani-pedi. Of course, she's very generous, so she always includes a nice tip for the nail technicians.

She doesn't think much about this monthly expense. She says that she and her daughter deserve to have this special time just for the two of them. Life is hard; they deserve this small monthly luxury.

But, I ask her, at what cost? She already had a very high credit card bill of $11,000 and the monthly trips to the nail salon were not helping to reduce that amount. She was only making the minimum required payment on the card, and adding to the balance all the time.

I knew that Delia wouldn't change her habits unless she really wanted to. No one, especially me, could force her to make such a drastic change in her spending habits.

The wake-up call came one day at the nail salon, when Delia and her daughter had just finished with their mani-pedis. She handed the cashier her credit card, and it was declined. She had maxed it out. Delia was shocked. She had no idea what to do. She had to pay for the services—she couldn't just walk out. This week happened to be the week she was paid, so she knew that there was money in her checking account. She took her debit card out of her wallet, and handed it to the cashier.

She successfully paid for the nail services, but now she knew that her checking account would have less money than it needed to. She had bills to pay and groceries to buy. That's when she came to me for help.

"Delia," I said, "I know you want to win with money. And you will! I have complete faith in you." I told her. "In the long run, you will have plenty of money to get your nails done. But for a short period of time you are going to have to give up a few things, so that later you can have whatever you want."

Delia stared at me—she did not like what I was saying.

"I work very hard, and my daughter and I deserve to do this fun thing once a month."

I agree with her. It's important to do fun things, and to have something to look forward to, for you and your children. It was simply time to make a choice.

Did she want to continue to rack up the bills, or did she want to get out of debt? She couldn't have it both ways. When we had first met and discussed the best way to save money, I explained how to set up a budget and how important it is to stick to that budget. We even discussed that it may be necessary to give up some luxuries for the short term, in order to win long term.

When you are told by someone that you need to give up the things that are important to you, the things that you love, it's natural to not want to listen. If your daily treat to yourself is a grande caramel latte from Starbuck's, you don't want to listen when you're told to make your coffee at home. If it's suggested that you start brown-bagging it to your work place, you will not enjoy giving up that lunch time burger.

Single parents really are super-heroes. I believe that with all my heart. You have to do it all. You have strength, energy, and will-power that many people don't. And that's why I will continue to encourage you to let go of these costly luxuries in order to get out of debt and have money in the bank. There is no better feeling than knowing you don't have a maxed out credit card—you don't have any credit card debt at all. If there is an unexpected auto repair or medical bill, it's okay. You have the money in your emergency fund, and you don't have go into debt in order to pay for these things.

But it takes time to get there, and you will need to give up certain things.

I decided to run an idea by Delia that would help her financial situation, yet still provide the feeling of treating herself and her daughter. Instead of spending $200 at a salon, they could have a DIY salon at home. They could paint their nails while watching a fun movie together. Delia could research facial recipes online, and treat their pores with yogurt and avocados. She told me she would give it a try.

Maybe your expensive treat is not a monthly manicure, but a daily latte or cappuccino. You can easily make a delicious, high-end coffee drink at home. And, you don't need to buy an expensive machine that takes up counter space in order to steam your milk. There's a handy gadget available known as a "milk-frother." It looks like a tiny immersion blender, and when you put it in a cup of hot milk, it turns it into foamy goodness. I purchased several from Ikea, and I know they're also available on Amazon. Ikea sells them for less than three dollars.

Regarding coffee, I'm a firm believer that the best coffee is made with a French press, and not a drip coffee maker, or a one-cup-at-a-time coffee maker. Talk about expensive coffee! Those little plastic cups cost a lot of money and needlessly contribute to landfills.

If you have a French press and a milk-frother, along with your choice of flavor syrups, I guarantee that you will make a cup of coffee that will rival the flavor of any five-dollar concoction. You can buy a French press at TJ Maxx for $20. Those little coffee pots make the best coffee in the world.

Let's talk about cable. Have you "cut the cord?" So many people are moving in that direction. Every year, the cable companies raise their rates and there's nothing you can do about it. Your kids want Disney and Nickelodeon, and you can't live without the Food Network. But you know what? You can. Many cable bills cost around $200 a month. That's $200 that could be going toward paying off debt, or building savings. Is it really necessary to spend so much money on television? Aren't there better ways to spend your money, and your time? Don't get me wrong; I love a good horror movie, and many of the BBC shows are my favorites. But I don't need cable to enjoy these shows.

Many people today are dropping their cable television and their landline telephones. As long as you have a cell phone, you don't need a land line.

It makes much more sense to only have your Internet connection, and one or two television subscriptions (Netflix, Hulu, Amazon Prime, Roku, Sling, etc.) Cutting cable out of your life is an excellent way to save money.

"But what about our local channels?" you might ask. "I enjoy watching my local news."

You still can. Once you have cut the cable cord, you can usually still get your local channels over-the-air. You'll need to purchase an antenna for these channels. It's an indoor antenna, not one of those ancient monstrosities that people used to mount on their roofs. These antennae mount on your wall and receive transmissions from the television stations over-the-air. This way, you'll still be able to watch your favorite local weatherman, and the shows on the network stations.

It may be a difficult choice to stop buying the thing you enjoy. That's okay. Doing the right thing is never easy. It's important to remember that cutting back is only temporary. Once you are successfully managing your budget, paying off debt, and saving for emergencies, you'll be able to add luxuries back into your budget. That is, of course, if you decide that you really, really miss cable. I have a hunch that you won't.

Action Plan

- Examine your expenses and find some items to cut from your budget.

Eating Out

"Dad, we wanna eat pizza tonight!" "Dad, can we go to McDonald's for dinner?"

I'm sure you hear those words about four times a week; maybe more. I know how incredibly difficult it is to provide home-cooked meals every night as a single parent. It's impossible. So, it makes perfect sense that you would rather swing by the drive-through after working all day, instead of cooking dinner.

The problem is that eating out multiple times each week can drain your bank account very quickly. And, eating out frequently just isn't very healthy.

Paul, a single dad who frequently attended our single parent events, realized that he was spending too much money at restaurants. When Paul's son was with him they ate out practically every night. It was fast and easy. He asked for my advice on the best way to save money, and also some tips on cooking at home.

I understand that not everyone is addicted to the Food Network. But that doesn't mean that you can't create simple and healthy meals for you and your family. Sometimes you just need an idea to get started. There are many online resources that can help.

For example, do you know how incredibly versatile a rotisserie chicken can be? Use it to make chicken fajitas or burritos. Throw it in some chicken stock with some veggies and egg noodles, to make chicken noodle soup.

Ground beef is also great to have on hand. Burgers, meatballs, and spaghetti sauce are usually big hits with kiddoes. Now, when I say spaghetti sauce, I don't mean the stuff out of a jar. It is easy, cheap, and delicious to make your own sauce. The beautiful thing is that you can make a big batch, and throw it in the freezer. Then, you can thaw and cook it when you're ready! I have included my go-to pasta sauce recipe in the back of this book. It's so easy, and so good. Enjoy!

When my kids were younger they would be so excited when we would have breakfast for dinner. And it's so easy—scrambled eggs, bacon, fruit, maybe a few pancakes. Your own kids will be thrilled.

I urged Paul not to be nervous. If he could work on only two or three recipes to get started, that would be plenty. He thought it would be easier for him if he prepared the same meal every Monday, Tuesday, Wednesday, etc. I told him that was just fine. So, Monday could be spaghetti and meat sauce day, and, of course, you must have Taco Tuesday. Ask your kids for their input when it comes to the meal schedule.

Cooking family meals can evolve into some wonderful quality time and memory making for you and your children. Cooking can be fun and rewarding, and it certainly is a valuable life skill. As you're preparing dinner for you and your family, include your children. Have them help you. If you're kiddoes are younger, they can assist by pouring ingredients into a saucepan, or measuring items. Teach them the different measurements that are used, such as tablespoons, teaspoons, and cups.

Older children can start learning knife skills, with proper supervision of course, and can help with stirring sauces on the stove.

Cooking meals at home, instead of dining out frequently, is one of the best ways to save money and eating real food is healthier and tastier than take-out.

Now, of course, everyone wants to order a pizza occasionally, or enjoy a restaurant meal. But this should be more of a treat than an everyday occurrence. That's where the Dining envelope comes in. We learned about using envelopes earlier—we only use the money in each envelope to buy the items in that category. If the clothing envelope is empty, you can't buy any clothes.

The Dining envelope is perfect for deciding whether or not you can go out to eat. The next time your kids say, "Dad, can we go to McDonald's tonight?" just tell them to check the Dining envelope, and see if there's any money in it. It's so much easier for kids to understand the value of money when they can actually see it. If you simply say, "No, we can't go out to eat because we don't have enough money," it's difficult for them to picture that. You know that there isn't enough money in your checking account, but kids don't get that. Allowing them to see the amount of money that is in the envelope, allocated specifically for dining purposes, helps them understand if you can go out to eat, or if it's breakfast-for-dinner.

But make sure they understand that the envelope situation is temporary! That's the wonderful thing about payday. When payday rolls around again, the envelope will be replenished, and you can plan for a delivery pizza, or an outing at McDonald's.

Easy Weekday Meals

Here's the thing—the tough part of putting dinner on the table every night is not the act of preparing and cooking. The tough part is figuring out what the heck you're going to feed those munchkins who only want to eat chicken nuggets and PopTarts.

You don't have to spend hours slaving over a hot stove in order to feed your kiddoes a tasty, healthy, inexpensive dinner.

Make-Ahead

If you can complete just a little bit of meal-prep on the weekend, you'll save a lot of time during the week, when you're helping with homework, looking for cleats, and getting dinner on the table all at the same time.

Check out these tips:

1. A rotisserie chicken can be a life saver. It's already cooked, the meat falls off the bones, and you can use cooked chicken meat for many different meals.
2. Cook a large-ish batch of rice on the weekend—that way, you'll just need to heat it up at dinner time.
3. An alternative to the rotisserie chicken is a batch of grilled chicken breasts.

Recipes from My Friends

Quesadilla

Every culture has its own version of a quesadilla—cheese and bread. Who doesn't love pizza or a grilled cheese sandwich? A quesadilla is just as tasty and so easy to spice up.

- Flour tortillas
- Shredded cheese
- Chopped, cooked chicken (optional)
- Salsa (optional)
- Sour cream (optional)
- Avocado/guacamole (optional)
- Sliced or diced tomatoes (optional)

Place the desired amount of cheese on one tortilla. Make sure it's spread around evenly. If you're using chicken, add that on top of the cheese. Cover it with another tortilla. Use a large spatula to carefully lift the quesadilla and place it in a pre-heated skillet on the stovetop. Cook on medium low until the bottom tortilla is light brown. Flip and continue cooking until the other side is light brown. Cover the skillet to help the cheese melt.

Serve with your choice of condiments.

Pasta Sauce

Homemade pasta sauce is easy and delicious. Make a batch or two, divide the sauce into containers, then throw them in the freezer. It'll defrost quickly, so you don't have to plan too far ahead.

Here's what you'll need:

- Two 14 ounce cans tomatoes
- Half an onion
- Two cloves chopped garlic
- One teaspoon salt
- One half teaspoon black pepper
- One tablespoon dried parsley
- One teaspoon dried basil

If you prefer different spices, or maybe a little more garlic, that's fine. Change it up! This is a simple, delicious recipe that you can make your own.

Instructions

- Heat a couple tablespoons of olive oil in a heavy skillet or pot.
- Rough-chop the onion, add it to the pan, and sauté over medium/medium low heat, until it's soft and translucent.
- Add the garlic, and sauté just for a couple minutes. Watch that the garlic doesn't burn.
- Add the two cans of tomatoes and the spices.
- If you think it's a little too thick, add a little water or stock.
- Simmer for about 15 or 20 minutes.

Give it a taste—if the sauce needs a little something extra, go ahead and add it.

Tip: My kids are not fans of chunky pasta sauce. If you have an immersion blender (or, as we call it, a stick blender) go ahead and blend the sauce until it's smooth.

Serve with your favorite pasta. It's also really easy to add frozen meatballs to the sauce. They cook quickly, and kids love meatballs.

Breakfast for Dinner

Who doesn't love Breakfast for Dinner? When my kids were little, this was a real treat. You might be thinking, "Cereal! I can do that!" But, come on, let's be a little more creative. Here are some tasty breakfast ideas:

- Bacon and Cheesy Scrambled Eggs
- Waffles
- Pancakes
- Toast
- Fresh Fruit
- Yogurt

Grilled Cheese

A crispy, melty grilled cheese sandwich is still one of my favorites, and my kids have always loved them, too.

Here's what you'll need:

- Two slices of your favorite bread
- A few slices of your favorite cheese
- One tablespoon-ish butter

Place the cheese inside the two slices of bread. Melt the butter in a skillet over medium to medium-low heat. Place the sandwich in the skillet, and cover the skillet.

Keep a close eye on the sandwich, so the bread doesn't burn. When the bottom of the sandwich is golden-brown, use a spatula to flip the sandwich to the other side. Cover the skillet again, continuing to watch it, so it doesn't burn. When both sides are golden and crispy, and the cheese is gooey, your sandwich is ready.

Serve alone, or with a bowl of your favorite soup. Tomato soup is perfect for dipping.

Homemade Pizza

Making homemade pizza is so much fun for kids. They love to choose their toppings, and create their very own culinary creation. No more having to get cheese-only, because that's what Little Brother wants. It's all about them.

Here's what you'll need:

- Pizza crust—You can buy these already made, pre-made dough that is ready for baking, or you can make your own pizza crust dough.
- Pizza sauce—Just pick up a jar. Easy peazy.
- Cheese—The traditional pizza cheese is, of course, mozzarella. Use your favorite.
- Toppings—The sky's the limit! Let your kiddoes pick their favorite toppings, no matter how gross you think they are.

Grilled Fish

You might think that kids don't like fish. Of course, you know your kids best, so they may not. But I know a lot of kids these days who gobble down salmon, mahi-mahi, or tilapia. These mild fish are available frozen, in individually-sealed packages. They have no skin or bones. There's nothing gross about these gorgeous fillets.

The easiest and tastiest way to prepare the fish is in an air fryer. You can certainly throw them in the oven, but the air fryer is so quick and easy, and the circulating air cooks the fish perfectly.

To thaw the frozen fish, place the still sealed fillet in a bowl filled with lukewarm water. It won't take long to defrost the fish.

When thawed, cut the plastic wrapping open and remove the fish from the plastic. Brush the fish with some olive oil, and season with salt and pepper. Cook according to your air fryer's directions.

Serve with your kids' favorite condiments—lemon juice, ketchup, sriracha, etc.

Action Plan

- Find some simple, tasty recipes that you can make at home.
- Make sure you have a Dining envelope.

New vs. Used (Consignment, Cars)

Appliances

Gloria was ticked off. Her oven quit working again. This was the third time this month, and she needed it. She had promised to bake a batch of lemon squares for the non-profit organization she volunteered for. A friend of hers had tried to fix it, but it never stayed fixed. She was afraid that she was going to be forced to buy a new oven.

Gloria had two young children. She had been working hard to pay off the debt left over from her divorce, and start putting money into an emergency fund. She certainly didn't need this headache right now. How much would a new wall oven cost, anyway? She opened a browser on her laptop, and performed a quick search at the various big-box shops.

The least expensive ovens listed were $700! She wasn't going to pay that much.

"Deep breaths," she told herself. "Do not freak out."

Gloria really just wanted an oven that would work. It didn't matter whether or not it was brand new—it needed to get hot and stay hot for a pre-determined amount of time. So, if she didn't need a brand spanking new oven, where should go? She could try her local Facebook Marketplace.

She brought up the classified site for her area, and entered the maximum price as $200. The screen in front of her displayed about ten results. She hit the jackpot!

I have believed for many years that there's nothing wrong with buying used items. Many people buy new, then decide they would rather have something different. So, the items they purchased are still in perfect working order, and they are listed for sale.

Or, someone might buy a home and decide to do a little remodeling. The appliances that were in the house are now listed on Facebook.

Just a word of caution—if you decide to purchase an item listed anywhere online, whether it's Craig's List, Facebook, or any other site, do not go to someone's home by yourself. Either take someone with you, or meet the seller in a neutral, busy location. Be careful.

My kitchen needs a complete remodel. It needs the whole works—cabinets, countertops, appliances, sink, faucet, and backsplash. That is going to be expensive. I don't have the money for that right now, and I absolutely refuse to borrow money to remodel my kitchen. I will eventually save enough.

But, not long ago, the ice maker in my refrigerator quit. It just stopped. Instead of spending money on a new appliance, I decided to go "old-school" and buy some ice cube trays from Amazon. Guess what—they work! I did not need to fix my ice maker, and I certainly didn't need to buy a new fridge, just because of a few little ice cubes. My old fridge still has some life left, and the ice trays won't stop working.

I did look into repairing the ice maker. I'm a big believer that just because a part of an appliance fails, it doesn't mean you need to replace the whole dang thing. YouTube provides videos on how to fix just about anything. You can buy replacement parts online. It's not difficult to keep an appliance running well for many years. In this situation, the replacement parts cost more than I wanted to pay.

I do understand that emergencies will happen. Ovens will die, parts will go out and can't be replaced. Before rushing to your nearest hardware or big-box store, research the used items that are available in your area.

Cars

There is a myth in this country that new cars are more reliable than used ones. Once a car has traveled about 100,000 miles, many people think it just doesn't have any life left. Time to trade it in. And, by trade it in, I mean take the car to a dealership, hand it over to them, and most likely finance a new car through that dealership.

I've known Carrie for quite a few years. When we met, she had been a single mom for a while, and her kids were in high school. Now, she's a happy empty-nester, with one adorable little grandson. Carrie has a great job as a real estate agent.

She had been leasing a car for about two years. Now, let's take a quick step back for a moment. Carrie did not own her car; she was leasing it. How, exactly, does a car lease work? When you lease a new car from a dealer, you are basically renting that car for a certain amount of time. You are required to maintain that vehicle, just as if you had purchased it. At the end of the lease, you need to turn it back in to the dealer, or you have the option of buying the car.

People are attracted to a lease because the monthly payment is often lower than the payment would be if you were to purchase a new, off-the-lot car and finance that purchase.

I've heard people say, "I'll have a car payment for the rest of my life, anyway! I'll just get a new car every two years!"

According to a Huffington Post article from March 2017 the average car payment in America is a whopping $493. By leasing a car, the payment is a bit lower at $412.

When you lease a car, you may think you're not paying any interest since you didn't specifically "borrow" any money. You're used to paying interest on a loan for something you buy, right? And since you don't "own" this car, you're not paying any interest; just kind of a rental fee. Wrong.

You are paying interest on the MSRP, or sticker price, of the vehicle. On top of that, you're paying a leasing, or finance, charge.

What you need to keep in mind is that if you don't have a car or lease payment, you actually have MONEY.

When Carrie told me that she really didn't like her car, and wanted to get rid of it, I was excited for her. I was thinking she could make a great financial decision and buy a used car, with lower (or no) payments. Alas, my wish did not come true. Carrie decided to return her leased car early and purchase a brand new car, financed through the dealer.

Her reasons were sound. They made sense. I'm sure that many other people have thought the same things.

Myth #1
"I won't buy a used car because I don't want to buy someone else's problems."

Absolutely, there are some used cars that are pieces of crap. That is completely true. And, there are some used cars that have been impeccably maintained over the years and run perfectly well. How can you make sure you're getting one of the good ones?

First, if you are shopping for a used car online at a site such as AutoTrader or Craig's List, make sure that the photos of the car display a real license plate, and not a paper, or temporary, plate. In most cases if the vehicle has a temporary plate, it's being sold by a car flipper. Just like the people on HGTV who flip houses, there are people who flip cars.

You don't want to buy a car from a flipper. These cars were purchased for a low price, maybe cleaned up a bit, and then listed at a higher price. You have no idea what is going on with these cars; there are no maintenance records, and there's probably something not-quite-right with it. They're just trying to make a quick buck.

But how can you tell? How do you know if the radiator hoses have recently been replaced, or if the muffler is about to fall off? If you're talking with the owner of the vehicle (which you should be) ask them for all of the maintenance records; or, at least the ones that they have. While some people may keep these, others may not. The seller may not have a receipt for every oil change, but they really should have the records of the large repairs that were done on the car.

Now, if they don't, that doesn't necessarily mean that you should walk away. The maintenance records are more of a nice-to-have than a have-to-have. The have-to-have is taking the car to a mechanic that you trust, who will perform a thorough inspection and let you know everything that is right and wrong with the car. Some issues may be minor, and don't have to be repaired or replaced right away. Other issues could be very expensive. No matter what the issues are, your mechanic will be able to tell you if the car is sound, and if it's worth the price that the seller is asking.

You should find a local mechanic that is recommended by your friends, family, or neighbors. Put out a call on Facebook or on your Nextdoor site for mechanic recommendations. Be sure to check Yelp and Google reviews. But, take the reviews with a grain of salt. Do you think the negative ones are accurate, or were they written by someone who was just really upset?

A local mechanic who works on all makes of cars is preferable to using a dealer for repairs. The service departments of dealerships tend to charge more than an independent mechanic. And, it's great to develop a relationship with your neighborhood car repair guys and gals.

The cost for having a car inspected prior to purchase is usually under $100, which is an excellent investment. There are some shops that don't charge anything for this service—they use it as a relationship builder to get to know you, and to earn your trust and your business.

"But," you may ask, "what if the seller won't let me take the car to a mechanic to have it checked out?"

That's when you walk away. Most sellers understand that savvy buyers will insist on having the car inspected before agreeing to a purchase. If they don't agree, then they're most likely hiding something. Don't worry about walking away from a car—there will always be another one.

Myth #2
"The cost to repair a used car will be more than the cost of a new car."

There are components of a car that will fail with time. It's called "wear and tear" and it's unavoidable. Everyone needs to perform regular maintenance on their vehicle in order to keep it in tip-top shape.

It's just like going to the dentist twice a year for a regular check-up and cleaning. With regular brushing, flossing, and dental cleanings, you're able to stay on top of your dental health, and take care of any issues while they're still minor, and easy to deal with. It's the same thing with your car.

The most important type of preventive maintenance you can do for your car is to have regular oil changes. This will help prolong the life of the engine. And, while you're there having the oil changed, the mechanics can also let you know if anything else needs a little help.

But, of course, parts and pieces will need to be replaced sometimes. That's why it's so important to have an emergency fund, or a **Car Repair** envelope. Think about how much money you might need to spend on car repairs in one year. Maybe $2,000? Perhaps $3,000? That might seem like a great deal of money, but it isn't if you divide the full amount by twelve months. For example, if you decide to have an annual car repair budget of $2,500 (we'll just split the difference) that means you'll need to save $208 each month. That is a lot less than the average American car payment!

If you are already accustomed to having a car payment in the $450 range, I suggest saving that entire amount each month. This will ensure that you are able to cover any unexpected repairs, and also provide a sum of money for when you need to purchase another new-to-you vehicle.

Again, if you are able to review the maintenance records that the seller has you'll have a good idea about the repairs that have already been done. If a radiator or water pump has been replaced, there's a very good chance that you won't need to have that done again for a long time.

Myth #3
"Once a car has 100,000 miles on it, it's finished."

I think this a myth that has been promoted in our country, just so dealers can sell new cars. I was 22 years old when I graduated from college, and I needed to buy a car. I had $2,000 to spend. The year was 1988 and as I was browsing the classified ads of my local newspaper I came across a 1981 Honda Accord. It was a four-door sedan with a five-speed. It was a lovely shade of green. And it had 95,000 miles on it.

With my dad's help, I asked the seller the right questions. He had maintenance records, and it appeared that he had taken good care of the Accord. My dad's mechanic agreed. Even with the high mileage it was a good car, and worth the $2,000 price tag. I was able to put another 100,000 miles on that little car. I wish I still had it.

As long as a car is well-maintained, it will have a productive, long life. Read the owner's manual and talk to your mechanic about the best way to take good care of your vehicle.

"My brand new car comes with free oil changes for a year and a warranty!"

Oh, that's great. So, how much does an oil change cost? On the high end, let's say about $60.00. You probably need to get the oil changed about three times each year. So, that's $180 that you've saved that first year. Awesome.

So, how much is that brand new car worth after owning it for one year? According to Carfax, a new car loses about 15% to 20% of its value in the first year. The first 10% is lost as soon as you drive it off the lot. Five minutes after you buy your $30,000 car, it's worth $27,000. One year later, it's worth $24,300 (an additional 10%). Don't forget, you're still making a car payment, which is most likely somewhere between $400 and $500 each month.

A well-maintained used car is truly the best bang for your buck.

Clothes

There is a small consignment shop in the town where I live. Women can bring the shop clothing that they no longer wear, and then they get a little cut of the sale price when someone buys their items. It's a win-win.

Shopping in a consignment store is like going on a treasure hunt. You never know what you'll find. It'll usually take a bit of digging, which is really kind of fun. The shop I visit is pretty small, so the clothing racks are very close together, and it can be a bit tough to move around. I go in about once a month to check out the inventory. Even though it's a bit crowded, the clothing is very well organized. I know that if I go to the section that says "medium" or "size 8," those are the sizes that I'll find.

I have found great brands, like Ann Taylor, Banana Republic, and Athleta. I don't think I've ever paid more than $10 for an item, and it's usually much less. A friend of mine once found a pair of (wait for it....) Christian Louboutin, complete with the red soles and the original shoe box! I think she paid $15 for them. You won't score a find like that every day, but you never know.

I recently discovered an online consignment shop, which I love just as much as the brick-and-mortar store. It's called ThredUp.com and the inventory is amazing. It's basically risk-free. If you order something that doesn't fit, or doesn't look like you thought it would, you can usually send it back.

I understand that some people are not fans of wearing clothes that have been worn before. I get that. In my opinion, that's what washing machines are for. I haven't run into anything that a little soap and water can't fix.

I've also made some great finds at Salvation Army and Goodwill stores. For your teens, see if there's a Plato's Closet in your area. They specialize in clothes for teens and tweens, and you can frequently get some great buys there.

People sell their clothing on consignment for many different reasons. It could be that the clothes simply don't fit anymore, or it's one of those items that have been sitting in their closet for so long, the owner finally comes to terms with the fact that they'll never wear it.

Visit your local consignment shop soon, and have some fun treasure hunting.

Action Plan

- When you need to make a purchase, don't be afraid to consider used.

What is Child Support?

In this chapter, I'm going to make some assumptions. They may be fair, or they may not be. I'll leave that up to you to decide.

When determining child support payments and amounts, the two parents are referred to as the Non-Custodial Parent (NCP) and the Custodial Parent (CP). The CP has primary custody of the children, and it's the CP's home where the kids spend most of their time. The kids also spend time with the NCP, but maybe not quite as much as with the CP. The NCP typically pays child support to the CP.

In most cases the NCP is the dad, and the CP is the mom. I understand that there are more and more single dads today whose children live with them full-time. In that case, they would be the CP, and Mom should be paying child support to Dad. Just to keep things a little more simple in this chapter, we are going to refer to the CP as "Mom" and the NCP as "Dad."

Let's start by determining what child support is, in the first place. I recently saw a tweet by someone that stated something similar to the following:

> *Child support payments should be automatically placed into an account until the child is eighteen.*

Apparently, this person believes that child support should be used as a savings account that the kiddo can use when he or she becomes an adult. It could even be part of a college savings program. But that is not what child support is meant for.

According to the Texas Office of the Attorney General, this is the definition of child support:

> *Financial support paid by a parent to help support a child or children of whom they do not have custody. Child support can be entered into voluntarily or ordered by a court or a properly empowered administrative agency, depending on each State's laws.*

This quote states that the payments are meant to help support a child or children. The money isn't supposed to go into a savings account. It's supposed to help pay for food, shelter, and clothing while the child is growing. Raising kids is expensive—everyone knows that. And, did you know that medical expenses and extra-curricular expenses are most often in addition to child support payments?

Child support is a moral and financial obligation by the non-custodial parent (NCP) to the custodial parent (CP). Every state has a different formula that determines the amount of child support that should be paid. Some states take into account the income earned by both parents. Other states simply assign a percentage of the NCP's income as the monthly child support payment.

This is a very tough topic. Many parents don't think the methods for calculating the payment amounts are fair. The NCP thinks the payments are enormous, and the CP often wonders when the money will show up. The bottom line is that the child support payment is meant to help pay for the welfare of the children. It helps pay the rent or mortgage for the home where the children live. It helps pay for groceries, heat, and air conditioning.

A male friend of mine told me once, "If my wife and I split up, I think that it would be financially easier on me. I can handle the child support payment, but raising two boys is very expensive. I think the child support would only cover a fraction of the actual expenses."

This was a very insightful observation by a man who had been happily married for over twenty years. And, it's completely true. Even though the monthly child support payment may seem like a lot to the NCP, it costs much more money to run the household where the children live most of the time, with the CP.

One question that frequently comes up, is whether or not the child support payment should be included in the monthly budget. My answer is "Yes" and "No." I know—that's not very helpful. Let me explain.

If you are the NCP and you are required to pay child support, then yes, of course you should include the payment in your monthly budget. If it's easier for you to break up the payment into two separate chunks, one portion that comes out of each paycheck, then go ahead and do that. Just make sure that you make the payment every month, like you were ordered to do by the court. It's for the benefit of your children.

If you are the CP and you are receiving the child support payments, then you should absolutely NOT count on it as a guaranteed part of your monthly income. Make sure that you can pay your bills on your income alone. Make sure that your rent or mortgage payment is in line with your income. When you do receive the child support payment, consider it gravy. Use it to pay down your debt, contribute to your emergency fund, or put it in an account for your children.

I realize that this goes against what I said previously about the purpose of child support. Yes, of course, it is meant to help raise your children, and pay for their necessities. But if a CP counts on that money in order to make the rent payment every month, and isn't able to do so if that money does not arrive, it's a big problem.

So, yes, of course, the child support payments must be paid. They should be paid. The NCP would happily make these payments, in order to do what's best for their child, right? And, don't forget, if the NCP was ordered by the court to pay child support, then they need to pay it, right? There are consequences for people who don't pay.

The Custodial Parent

That's exactly what Katie thought. She received right around $500 a month in child support from her ex-husband. He paid consistently for three years, and she included that amount in her monthly budget, as part of her regular income.

Then, out of the blue, Katie's husband lost his job. It wasn't his fault—he was caught up in a lay off that affected many people in his company. So, he stopped paying child support. Legally, of course, he wasn't supposed to do that. But, different states have different laws regarding child support, and the penalties are usually not too severe for the first one or two missed payments. An arrears balance would most likely begin accumulating.

This was a huge blow for Katie. She was devastated. That $500 every month was an integral part of her budget, and she was going to be late with several payments due to the lack of this money. She tried talking to her ex, and explained how she needed the money in order to stay afloat. He was sympathetic, but he told her that there was no way he could help her at that time. He was surviving only on unemployment benefits and his small savings account. He assured her that he was busy applying for multiple jobs every day, but he had nothing extra to give her at the moment.

Katie was panicked. She called the child support services in her state, begging for help. They explained that after the first month of non-payment, they would send her ex a sternly-worded letter. After the second month, he would receive another letter, explaining that he was in danger of losing his driver's license. When the third month rolled around, they would suspend his license. None of these actions would help Katie pay her bills.

If there is an arrears balance due, then one method of repayment is known as "Tax Refund Interception." When the NCP files his taxes and if he is due to receive a refund, the state child support office can take control of that refund, and apply it to the arrears. Unfortunately, these measures would not help Katie with her immediate financial needs.

The Non-Custodial Parent

David was an NCP with two daughters who lived with his ex-wife. He was a super-involved dad, and he really did his best to keep the girls' best interests at the heart of everything he did. He always made sure that the child support payment was made on time. David was even happy to give them extra money for clothes, school supplies, and anything else they needed.

Unfortunately, he didn't get along with his ex-wife very well. When they were married they had never agreed on how to manage money, which was a major factor in their divorce. David was not convinced that the child support that he made sure he paid exactly when it was due, was being used in a way that was best for his daughters.

The girls were always talking about the new clothes that their mom bought (for herself, not for them), the restaurants she frequented, and how perfect her nails looked. David was annoyed, but he knew that there was nothing he could do about it. Once he made the payment, he had no control over how his ex-wife spent the money.

This doesn't sound fair. One would think that there would be some rules or guidelines as to how child support money should be spent. Unfortunately, that would be very difficult to control, so it is left up to the Custodial Parent to determine the best way to use the money.

Action Plan

- If you're the Custodial Parent, *do not* add child support to your monthly budget as regular income.
- If you're the Non-Custodial Parents, *do* add the child support payment to your monthly budget as a regular expense.

Credit

Credit is dangerous. When I divorced in 2005 my ex-husband and I had $80,000 in credit card debt. We agreed to split that in half, so we each needed to repay $40,000. My ex decided to file for bankruptcy. This was something I felt very strongly about NOT doing. I understand that there are some situations where filing bankruptcy is the best option. Sometimes unforeseen medical expenses caused by a catastrophic accident can be so overwhelming that you need to file bankruptcy.

In my case, I believed that my credit card debt was my fault. I needed to pay back the money that I had borrowed.

Credit is dangerous because it's easy to get in over your head. It's much too easy to swipe that card, and not think about the bill that will show up later in the month.

But credit is also an important part of the financial system in which we live today. Your credit score will determine interest rates, insurance rates, and sometimes even whether or not you'll be considered for a job.

We had so much credit card debt because we were living on credit for about two years. I was home taking care of our children and our home, and my ex was trying to get a business up and running. We had hardly any income; just enough to make the minimum payments on everything.

When I went grocery shopping for my family, I had to charge the cost of the groceries on a credit card. I will never forget the horrible feeling of standing at the cash register, swiping that card. I had a terrible, sick feeling in my stomach. I knew that I was charging more and more on my credit card, and I had no idea how I was going to pay it off.

I remember going to bed very early each night, and waking around two in the morning. I wasn't able to get back to sleep for hours. I stayed up worrying, and wondering how this mess was ever going to be cleaned up.

When you're right in the middle of a difficult time in your life, it can be tough to imagine the resolution. It took me a while to pay off the debt and accumulate some savings, but once I found a plan that worked for me, and I stuck to it, I started to see the progress.

Once I emerged from that depressing period of my life, I vowed to never again put myself in a situation like that. I would only buy things that I could afford to pay for with cash. If I needed to borrow money to pay for something, I just didn't need it that badly.

Credit Cards

There is a smart way to use credit cards. In order to raise your credit score, and keep it high, you should have one credit card with a fairly low limit. Keep the credit limit at about $500 or $1,000. In order to maintain a good score, you don't need a high limit on your credit card. And you won't be tempted to buy things you really can't afford.

Use your card for relatively small bills that you have to pay for every month. Pay for your cell phone using your card and **pay it off every month**. Pay for the gas for your car using your credit card and **pay it off every month**. Pay for some groceries with your card and **pay it off every month**.

Can you see where I'm going with this?

Do not carry a balance on your credit card. You want to make sure that you pay it off every month. This is how you can achieve a high credit score, and keep it high, without getting into trouble by accumulating debt.

So, what exactly is a credit score, and what determines whether your score is high or low?

Your credit score, or FICO score, typically ranges from 300 to 850. Anything over 700 is considered a very good score. Few people have a score around 800, but it is possible to achieve that.

The following factors play into your score:

- Payment History (35%)—This is the largest factor in your FICO score. Credit Bureaus want to see that you do not carry a balance on your credit card, and that you make payments on time, every time.

- Amounts Owed (30%) —This factor is your debt vs. credit limit. Credit Bureaus want to make sure you're not maxing out your cards, and borrowing as much as you possibly can.

- Length of Credit History (15%) —While not as important as the first two factors, the longer you have a credit history, the higher your score should be. It makes sense that for a young person just beginning their financial journey, the score will be a bit lower than the score of an older person.

- New Credit and Types of Credit Used make up the final 20% of the FICO score. In my opinion, this factor is not as important as your payment history and amounts owed.

As I said previously, one credit card is all you need. Use that card to charge a few regular monthly expenses that you have; gas for the car, cell phone, maybe some groceries. Pay it off every month.

I know that not everyone will agree with me. I've heard people say that you need to have multiple credit card accounts open, even if you don't use them. I've also heard that you're supposed to carry a balance on your credit card and not pay it off each month. That is absurd.

Shannon is a woman I work with, and she has a grown son named Zach. Zach is around 30 years old now, and a successful software developer, living in Arizona. When he first began his adult life he asked his mom's advice regarding credit cards, and how to build your credit score. Shannon is smart. She advised him to do exactly what I've recommended.

She told him to have one credit card, charge a few things, and pay it off every month. That's what he's done for the last ten years. During that time, Zach has never bought a house (he's a renter), and never taken out a loan of any kind. He drives a very old Toyota that his grandma had given him.

With this kind of credit history and only one credit card, Zach's FICO score is just under 800. That is an excellent credit score. And, it's proof that this simple method works.

Credit Reports

You've heard about identity theft, right? Who hasn't? Everyone today is afraid that their social security number will be stolen. We're all certain that some shady character is opening many credit cards in our names, and charging thousands of dollars. While I'm being a bit facetious, this is certainly a legitimate concern today.

Identity theft is scary, and it can happen to anyone. It's vital that you are vigilant. You must know every checking and savings account you have open, and how much money is in each of those accounts. You must also know each credit account you have open. Identity thieves will frequently open credit accounts in your name.

When it comes to my bank accounts, I'm a little crazy. Every morning I log into my online bank account. I look at the balance of each account, and make sure that each account contains the transactions that I'm expecting.

Several years ago, as was being OCD (in a good way) and perusing the transactions in my main checking account, I noticed something that looked strange. There was a pending transaction that had occurred at 3:00am that morning. It was for a very small amount; only $1.50 but I didn't remember making that purchase from HobbyTown USA. I had no idea what that was. And at three o'clock in the morning? No way.

This is a trick that online thieves will use. Somehow (who knows how) someone got a hold of my debit card number. They used it to make a very small purchase. If a few days had gone by without my noticing this little transaction, then they would have continued to use my card to buy more expensive items. Since I'm in the habit of checking my accounts daily, I caught them in the act, and shut them down!

I immediately called my bank and let them know what happened. I wasn't responsible for that purchase, of course, and the money was refunded to my account. The bank also deactivated my debit card and issued a new one to me.

Monitoring your checking account is an easy way to make sure no one is using your debit card to make online purchases. But what about credit cards? How can you know if someone has used your personal information, like your social security number, to open a credit card in your name without your knowledge?

You can find this information on your credit report. Your credit report is maintained by the three main credit reporting bureaus. These are Equifax, TransUnion, and Experian. You can pull your full credit report from each of these agencies for free, once each year.

The easiest way to do this is by going to www.annualcreditreport.com and requesting your report.

Or, there's even an easier way! CreditKarma.com will show a snapshot of your credit score and all open accounts. Their information in updated continually. You can quickly view any loans or credit cards that are currently open in your name. If you see anything that does not look right, then you need to start looking into that right away.

Do you see a Capital One credit card account that you never opened? Call Capital One and find out what's going on! Tell them to close it immediately, and let them know you never opened that account. All credit card companies (and banks) have fraud departments. They will work with you.

Here's one point regarding CreditKarma; there are many credit card companies who advertise on this site. CreditKarma will frequently recommend that in order to raise your credit score, you need to open more credit card accounts. As we mentioned previously in this chapter, it can be dangerous to open too many credit card accounts. Stick with one, and pay it off every month.

Action Plan

- Use credit wisely—have one credit card, and pay it off every month.
- Review your credit report at least once each year.

Debt

Payments toward debt will eat up your paycheck before you have a chance to put anything in your saving account. Don't be ashamed for having debt—most people do. Your goal is to be different from the rest, and pay off your debts as quickly as you can. I use the word "quickly" loosely. It can take several years to eradicate your debt, and that's okay. You just need a plan in order to make progress.

You might be wondering why you should even worry about paying off your debt. If everyone has debt, what's the big deal? It's the American way of life.

Here's the truth—if you don't have any debt, and you're not making any payments toward debt, you will have MONEY. This is money that you can use toward everyday expenses, savings, and fun things for you and your family. This is what you should be using your money for. You shouldn't be giving it to some company or bank that you borrowed from. Use it to save for your future and to plan outings with your children. Save it to buy the things you need instead of getting financing from a huge furniture store.

The first thing you need to do is know exactly how much debt you have. Would you believe that many people have so many credit cards, student loans, personal loans, and little onesie-twosie debts that they don't even know the exact number that they owe?

Are you ready to start tackling your debt, and keeping your money? Good! Let's get started.

The first thing you need to do is get a handle on how much you owe. Now, when we're talking about paying off debt we're referring to consumer debt. If you own a home and have a mortgage payment, that isn't included in this step.

Consumer debt is all of your other debt, including student loans and car payments. Gather all of the statements for each of your loans. If you handle all of the payments electronically, log into each site. Find out exactly how much the balance of each debt is, how much your payment is each month, and the date that each payment is due. Use the worksheet at the end of this chapter to record every single debt. Add up the balances. Then you'll know exactly how much you need to tackle.

There are several different opinions when it comes to the best strategy for paying off debt, and determining which debt is paid off first. You absolutely need to select one, and tackle that first. Focus is everything. You can't focus on many debts at once. But which one do you start with?

The different opinions are:

- Start paying off the debt with the smallest balance.
- Start paying off the debt with the highest interest rate.

Whichever method you choose, you'll throw any extra money you have to the principal, or balance, of that debt. Get it paid off as quickly as you can, then move on to the next. While you are intensely tackling the first debt, you need to continue making the minimum payments on the others.

You'll need to be focused. You'll need to sacrifice. You'll need to understand that eradicating your debt will help you win with money in the long run.

Action Plan

- Use the worksheets to document your debts.

DEBT NUMBER ONE					
Starting Balance	Interest Rate	Minimum Payment	Payment Due Date	Actual Payment	Remaining Balance

DEBT NUMBER TWO					
Starting Balance	Interest Rate	Minimum Payment	Payment Due Date	Actual Payment	Remaining Balance

DEBT NUMBER THREE					
Starting Balance	Interest Rate	Minimum Payment	Payment Due Date	Actual Payment	Remaining Balance

Money and Kids

When I was growing up parents didn't talk to children about sex or money. Those topics were taboo. I never had any idea how much money my parents earned or how much things cost. Let's not even mention the lack of discussions regarding sex. That's another book.

When I was in high school my mother taught me how to balance a checkbook. She also encouraged me to apply for a department store credit card, which I did. But we never had any discussions about how to spend less money than you make, which is the best way to ensure that I'll be able to live within my means, and not go into debt.

I always knew that my parents were doing fine financially. I knew that they didn't have debt, and that there was money in a savings account. But no one ever explained to me how that was accomplished. They never explained to me how to make sure that I was spending less money than I was earning.

It's our job as parents to teach our children about money. There's a lot of talk these days about how schools are not teaching any life skills to our high school students. That may be true. While it would be great if the majority of high schools in our country were to teach budgeting and financial responsibility to our children, I'm not too upset that they don't. I really see teaching my children about money as my responsibility. I'm fine with that.

What does that look like? What does it mean to teach your kids about money? Now, teaching kids about money will be different at various stages in their lives. You can't teach a three-year-old how to balance a checkbook. But you can begin to teach her that money comes from working.

The envelope system is an excellent tool to help teach your kids about money at any age. When your three, seven, or twelve-year-old asks you for a special treat, it's very easy to show them the contents of an envelope.

As your children grow, you'll be able to share more about your own finances and teach them how money should be managed responsibly.

- Be Transparent—Tell your children how much money you make, and how much things cost. A lot of people have a problem with this. Parents think they're not supposed to tell their kids how much they earn. I've always wondered why that is. What is wrong with sharing your income with your own family? Maybe you're worried that they'll tell other people how much money you make. In this day of everything-you-ever-wanted-to-know is on the Internet, anyone can figure out how much the salary is for a particular profession in about two minutes. If you don't tell your kids what they can expect to earn when they have a full-time job, how will they know?

- Discuss the Budget—When my kids were teenagers I held monthly budget meetings. We sat down at the dining room table, and I showed them the budget and explained what was coming in, and what was going out. They teased me mercilessly and called me a nerd. But that was okay because they also knew how much things cost. They also saw, on paper, that I was not spending more money than I was earning.

- Allowance vs. Commission—Don't pay your children just for existing. Pay them for doing work, just like in the real world. Now, there are some things that kiddoes should simply be expected to do because they are a member of the family. Those items are up to you to decide what they should be. For the commission-based items, chore charts like the one on the following page can be incredibly useful.

Chore Chart

Name: _____
Week: _____

Tasks To Do	M	T	W	T	F	S	S
1.							
2.							
3.							
4.							
5.							
6.							
7.							
8.							

Filling the Void with Stuff

Stacey was racked with guilt over her divorce. She had stayed in a bad marriage for many years, believing that was the best thing for her son. Finally, she realized that it was worse for her son to see his mother and father in a marriage that was destructive. The constant fighting and belittling was damaging everyone. Stacey desperately needed some peace in her life, and she left.

Even though Stacey knew it was for the best, she was overwhelmed with guilt. She had been planning on sticking it out until her son, Jack, graduated from high school, believing that it's best for a child to live in a home with two parents, no matter what their relationship is like. Now she knows that isn't true.

Stacey and her ex-husband were actually doing pretty well with co-parenting, now that they didn't live together anymore. They both put Jack's best interests before their own. At this time he was eleven years old, and very busy with various activities. Both of his parents attended his baseball games, which is a healthy, excellent tradition for divorced parents to start.

Because of the responsibility she felt for changing Jack's life, she found it very difficult to say No to him. If there was a new video game that Jack wanted, Stacey bought it for him. The latest in baseball equipment? Jack had only to ask, and he received. Kids are smart; they figure out very quickly if a parent is likely to buy them something, and the best tactics to use in order to get what they want.

Jack knew that if he wanted a new bike and asked his father, he would be encouraged to either save his own money, or wait for the holidays or his birthday. But, if he asked his mom the same question, she was very likely to give in. Even if she didn't say Yes right away, he knew that he could eventually wear her down and get his way.

Stacey felt that if she told Jack No regarding something he wanted, she needed to provide him with an explanation. She needed to explain that he didn't need to go to the movies this afternoon because he had homework to do. Or, she wasn't going to buy that new video game, because $75 was a lot of money for a game, and she needed to buy other fun items, such as groceries.

So, if she started to tell him that he could not have a new toy that day, or get dinner at McDonald's that evening, he would simply start arguing with her, and explaining why he was right and she was wrong. He really became quite good at pleading his case. It was clear to see that law school would be in his future.

Due to Stacey's guilt about the divorce, and her complete inability to say No to her son, she was buying him everything he asked for. This presented two large problems: he was beginning to think that he was the boss in their household, and her credit card balance was rising.

Saying No is okay. It's not going to harm your child if you don't buy the latest and greatest thingamajig. And, guess what? No is a complete sentence. You are the parent, which means that you're the boss. You do not owe your kiddo an explanation for the decision you made. "Because I said so," is still an excellent response.

It's common for divorced parents to buy toys, games, sports equipment, etc. in order to try to make their children feel better. These parents mean well, of course. They believe that since they've taken away a two-parent home, they can replace it with paintball guns. We all understand the concept of trying to fill an emotional need with physical items. But this temporary fix can cause major problems down the road.

Our children need to understand that life is not all about having things. The number of toys that they have will not bring them happiness. And, before they can learn that, YOU need to learn that. Being content with what you have provides a tremendous feeling of peace, and well-being.

Spending time together is the best gift you can give your children. Do your best to co-parent with your ex, and let the kids watch you doing it. Let them have their friends over to your house; be the house where all the kids want to go, because they feel comfortable just hanging out. The secret to happiness is not about accumulating a bunch of stuff.

Action Plan

- Talk to your children about money.
- Teach your kids that money comes from working.

Money and Dating

Sarah, like many single moms, was interested in dating. She really wanted to meet someone who was different than her ex-husband. Obviously! Her two daughters visited their father every other weekend so that was when she had time to go out. She listed her profile on several of the matchmaking websites, and she met several nice men. She was taking things slowly because she was still a bit leery from her experiences in her marriage. Sarah and her ex-husband divorced mainly due to money fights and money problems. These issues happen to be the leading cause of divorce in the United States. Looking back, Sarah knew that from the beginning of their marriage she and her ex and had never agreed upon how to handle money. She knows now that they should have discussed this before they got married, but that didn't happen. Obviously, she didn't want to make the same mistakes again.

It is even more important to discuss money when you're in a relationship after a divorce. Not only do you want to avoid repeating mistakes made in the past, but when there are children involved you want to make extra sure that you and your new partner are on the same sheet of music.

Sarah started dating a man named Steve and things were moving along pretty well. He had a son from his first marriage and after about six months they decided to introduce their kids to each other. Sarah was very pleased because everyone seemed to be getting along very well. She and Steve had briefly discussed money in the past, and she decided that it was time to start asking him some questions.

It was a Saturday evening, and they were all in Steve's backyard getting ready to grill some steaks for dinner. The three kids were playing together in the pool, and Sarah and Steve were sitting at the patio table chatting, and watching the kids.

Sarah was not quite sure how to start this conversation, so she decided that direct way was the best.

"Steve," she began, "I'd like to talk about money."

He raised his eyebrows in surprise, but said, "Okay. What would you like to talk about?"

She was pleased with his response, and thought was a very good sign that he was willing to discuss the topic.

"Well," she began, "you know that I use the envelope system, and I live on a budget. I'd like to know how you handle your money. And, if you were to have a serious relationship again, how would you expect a couple to handle money together?"

This is a great way to open the door to a conversation about finances before getting married. It is so incredibly important to be on the same page as your spouse when it comes to money. One of you may be the spender and the other may be a saver, but as long as you have the same goals and are able to discuss your finances without fighting about them it will be okay.

But before we even get to the wedding day, we need to make sure that both parties agree. And that's going to take some discussion.

Before my new husband and I were married we had many, many conversations about money. He knew that I religiously used the envelope system and I wanted to make sure that he would still support that after we were married. I also wanted to make sure that he supported the idea of using a written budget every time we were paid. And, more importantly, sticking to that budget. I wanted to know that we had similar goals when it came to spending and to saving; specifically saving for retirement.

As a single parent, when you're considering joining two families it is vital to discuss how much money will be spent on each other's children. Many kids today are involved in many different activities that cost money. Gymnastics, baseball, ice skating, swim team, etc. Or, maybe your child is not involved in as many activities as your new spouse is children, and you don't agree with the amount of money that is being spent for their activities.

Again, these are topics and need to be discussed before the wedding day. In my situation, I have three children and my husband has none. Since we are married and we consider the money that I earn and the money that he earns to be "our" money, we needed to agree on how much money will be spent on my children.

If there is something that I would like to buy for one of my children, I typically talk to my husband about it first. I wouldn't call it "asking for permission," I simply believe it is respectful and necessary to talk to him about how our money is being spent.

I remember hearing from a woman named Patti. Patti was in her fifties and had been married to her new husband for about ten years. She had two grown children and three grandchildren. Patti absolutely loved set spending time with her kids and grandkids and also buying things for them. Her husband was not so thrilled with buying presents for the children.

She didn't think she wanted to spend a ridiculous amount on her family; maybe $50 here for some clothes, and she really wanted to pay for the monthly ice skating lessons for her youngest granddaughter. Those cost about $100 each month. She knew that these expenses were not that extravagant, and they could afford them. The problem was that her husband just didn't want to spend money on "her" kids.

Patti decided that what her husband didn't know wouldn't hurt him. You can imagine that the situation quickly spun out of control. She found a way around letting him know about the money she spent on her family. She opened up a credit card in her name only and charged the items that she bought for her children to this credit card. Her husband had no idea this credit card existed.

Before she knew it, Patti had accumulated close to $10,000 in credit card debt. She was terrified of telling her husband, but she knew she was in over her head.

There is a term for what Patti did; it's called "financial infidelity." It means spending money and having debt that your spouse is not aware of. She intentionally spent money on things that she knew he wouldn't approve of. Pattie hated saying, "No" to her kids, but she knew every time she charged something on that hidden credit card, that she was just digging a deeper hole for herself. She had no idea how she would ever get out.

I'm sure everyone can agree that what she did was wrong, especially since the amount of debt reached such a large sum.

However, this hidden debt was really a symptom of a larger problem. Patti and her husband were not on the same page when it came to handling money. They fought and argued about many different aspects of their money, not only how much to spend on the children. They fought about how much Patti spent on groceries, and how much her husband spent on his model train hobby. Those little trains can get expensive!

Having a budget that both people agree on will help avoid these arguments. Personally, I feel so fortunate that my new husband and I do not argue about our finances. I'm the one who creates the budget for each paycheck (twice each month) and I run it by him. At that time, we discuss any changes that need to be made for that particular pay cycle. Once we agree on the budget, then that's how we spend our money.

Now, that doesn't mean that if something comes up and a change needs to be made that we are super-strict and can't adjust the budget. We simply need to have a discussion, and see if that expenditure needs to happen now, or if it could wait until the next pay cycle.

The point I'd like you to take with you is that the budget is continually open for discussion. We don't fight about it, we chat about it. It's a wonderful, peaceful feeling to agree with your spouse or significant other about money.

Can money issues be fixed after you're already married? Of course they can, if both spouses are willing to work on the problem. Do yourself a favor and have the conversation before you're married.

Action Plan

- If you plan to get married, talk to your new spouse about money *before* you have the wedding. Make sure you're on the same page financially.

Gift Giving
(Holidays, Kids' Birthdays, Other Kids' Birthdays)

Children's Birthday Parties

Caroline has two children; her son is twelve, and her daughter is nine. They both enjoy school, and they frequently get together with classmates for playdates. Both children are also involved in extra-curricular activities. They are your typical busy twenty-first century kiddoes.

Caroline is fine with that. She wants her kids to be well-rounded, and well-socialized. She believes it's important for children to learn how to interact with others, and be kind. Those are great parenting goals to have! These personal skills will last her children for the rest of their lives.

Since the kids have a lot of friends, they are invited to a lot of birthday parties. Sometimes Caroline feels like she's taking one, or both, of the kids to a party every single weekend. It might take place at the friend's home, or it might be at a swimming pool, arcade, or other fun location.

No matter where the party takes place, Caroline needs to make sure that she buys a gift for the birthday boy or girl. She lives on a very tight budget, so surprises such as learning on Friday about a party that's happening on Saturday could easily put a dent in it.

Everyone has their own idea about the right amount to spend on a birthday gift for a child's party. Caroline believed the sweet spot was between $10 and $20. She occasionally bought gift cards, but that was only if she was really in a bind. She preferred to get a few ideas from her own kids, or even the other child's parent, about their likes and dislikes. She especially loved being able to get a great item that was on sale, so it was still within her spending limit.

So, how does Caroline manage to pay for this outrageous number of birthday gifts? She has an envelope, of course! Every time she gets paid, she puts $20 into the Birthday Gifts envelope. She even does this during the summer months when her kids are not in school, just to make sure that she's never caught short.

I remember those days. When I had three kids in school, they were also going to birthday parties all the time. Before I discovered the magic of the envelope system, there were several times that I felt stuck between a rock and a hard place. I was short on money for a birthday gift, but I did not want to disappoint my child, or the birthday child. I may have charged a gift or two on a credit card.

I'm not kidding when I call the envelope system "magical." With just a little planning and envelope stuffing, a whole boatload of stress just vanishes. Poof! It's gone! There are no tears, no tantrums, and no credit card charges.

Your Child's Birthday

Now that we've discussed other kids' birthdays, let's talk about your own children. They want the latest and greatest gadgets, and the coolest parties. Sure, you could go to a local gymnastics center and they'll do all the work for you. Or, you can have a party at home, with burgers and cake.

It might not be trendy to have birthday parties at your own home anymore but it can be a great way to celebrate, and of course it's more cost effective. You can easily purchase decorations at your local dollar store and throw some burgers on the grill.

Again, we'll need to start by setting some spending limits. This will be a little different because you're probably buying a gift, and also planning a party. Or….are you? I remember the year my daughter turned sixteen. Ah…..Sweet Sixteen! You might be imagining party dresses, high heels, and lots of make-up. No. She wanted a paintball party.

It was the middle of January in Texas. Not too cold, but it ended up being a wet and muddy day. The local paintball field was outside, and all twelve of the young ladies (and one or two little brothers) had a blast. After a few hours of shooting each other in the mud, they came back to my house for queso and cake.

It was a great day, although a bit muddy, but it wasn't cheap. My daughter and I discussed the cost of the party, and also a possible tangible gift. Which "thing" did she want, and what would the cost be compared to the cost of the party?

We decided together that the experience of a really fun party was worth more than a trinket or a gadget that she would probably lose interest in after a few months. It was a great conversation to have with my almost 16-year-old. Without sounding like a lecture (we were just party planning) I was able to teach her about the value of memories and experiences. We also had a great adult conversation about how much to spend on a party, how to pay cash for it, and how everyone can have a great time without going overboard.

Christmas and Major Holidays

Earlier in this book we discussed setting a spending limit when it comes to buying holiday gifts for your children. I mentioned that I set a limit of $100 per child, and I tell them that so they know what to expect. The Christmas envelope actually brings up another point about buying gifts for the holidays. How many family members, friends, and acquaintances will you buy gifts for? Many of us believe that we need to go all out and buy extravagant gifts from everyone to the receptionist in our office to our mail carrier. That is a very generous spirit! However, it might not be possible to be quite so generous while you're working hard to pay off debt, and build a savings account.

$10? $25? $50?

It might be tough to reduce the amount of spending you might like to do during the holidays. We all see the sparkly advertisements, and practically everything is on SALE! How could you possibly pass up those leather gloves when they're 40% off? You don't have to, as long as those gloves are within your spending budget. But, then again, you might have to. Be strong!

There are certainly ways that you can give inexpensive gifts, such as a homemade cookies or candies. These types of gifts will cost more time than money. Creating gifts from the heart for family members and friends can be a beautiful way to spend time with your children!

How many ideas for creative, inexpensive, homemade gifts do you think you could find on Pinterest? One or two, maybe? Involve your children in the quest for perfect simple gifts. They'll find cookie mixes in a jar, transformed terra cotta flower pots, and wooden signs that carry special messages to dear friends. And much, much more.

As I performed research for this chapter of the book (Googling homemade Christmas gifts) I found some amazing ideas that are getting me excited to try something creative! I especially love the homemade soaps and coffee mugs with animal stencils on them. I'm so grateful for so many creative people who simply tell me how to make delicious and gorgeous trinkets!

When sending your kids off on this treasure hunt, make sure they understand that they will be involved with the making of the gifts. If they express interest in a craft that you're not familiar with, let them try it! You might have a blossoming woodworker or calligrapher in your midst.

It is also perfectly reasonable to tell your family, including adult siblings and parents, that you aren't able to buy expensive gifts. They will most likely appreciate your input, and be happy that they don't have to buy so many gifts, either! Many families today decide together that the adults don't need to exchange presents for the holidays.

The kids, of course, are a different story. Everyone wants to make sure that the children receive their presents. This can get pricey, too! If you have two or three siblings, and they each have two or three children, that could be up to nine nieces and nephews! Add that to your own children, and everyone is spending a lot of money on Christmas!

Again, have a conversation with your family. One solution is to draw names; throw the names of all the kids in a hat, and the adults can choose who they're buying for. This way, the kiddoes will get something extra from family, in addition to those Santa presents.

This is an idea that the grandparents will probably love. Many older people are on a fixed income. No one knows better than Grammy and Gramps, how expensive buying all of those toys, clothes, and electronics can be. They also know that the best part of the holidays is not the presents; it's the time you get to spend with your favorite people in the world.

On that note, if your family is really adventurous, they might be interested in doing something totally crazy; completely insane! What could I possibly be referring to? Zip-lining? Bungee jumping? Maybe a holiday cruise? No; something even crazier!

Since Christmas is about giving and spending time with the people you love, consider giving Christmas to a family who otherwise wouldn't have one.

In every town, there are "Angel Trees" which allow you to pull an ornament or tag from a tree, that contains a list of items that a family would love to have for Christmas. These families wouldn't have any presents if it weren't for the Angel Trees.

Start a tradition with your own family to adopt someone who otherwise wouldn't have a Merry Christmas.

Action Plan

- Talk to your family about cutting back on gift-giving.
- Don't feel bad about it!
- Help someone else have a Merry Christmas.

We all want to give our children everything their hearts desire. We want to buy gifts for our friends and family members. For most people, whether they are single, married, or single parents, that is not possible. We MUST put spending limits on the gifts we buy.

Saving

When I was growing up in my parents' home I knew that they were doing just fine financially. I didn't know how they did it, but I knew that there was little (if any) debt and that my parents had money in savings. Mom wasn't really a coupon clipper. She had the freedom to buy what she wanted at the grocery store without worrying too much about prices.

Dinner on Sunday was always a big deal. My parents planned and cooked it together, which I think is lovely. They spent all morning preparing, and it was ready to go by two or three o'clock in the afternoon. I know now, although I didn't realize it then, that the food they purchased to cook those Sunday dinners was very high quality. And that isn't cheap.

But because they had no debt, money in savings, and were living on less than they earned, they were able to buy really yummy groceries!

We all know that saving money is important. But, what are we actually saving for? Why have money in the bank? There are two main reasons that you should start saving as soon as you can.

These are:

- Emergency Fund
- Retirement

Now, believe or not, these two saving vehicles are more important than saving for your kids' college. Now, I know that might sound shocking, but it's true! YOU are the one who will have to pay for that car repair, or possibly a new water heater for your home. You are also the one who is ultimately responsible for making sure you have enough money when it's time to retire. Do not count on Social Security to cover all of your expenses.

So, let's dig a little deeper into these necessary savings vehicles.

Emergency Fund

According to a 2017 survey by **GOBankingRates**, 57% of Americans have less than, or right around, $1,000 in a savings account. A medical or automobile related emergency will consume the majority of that $1,000 in no time. If that account ends up being depleted, what happens then? Most people will charge their next emergency on a credit card, and never replenish the savings account. It becomes a nasty downward spiral.

That's why it's so important to make sure that you have enough money in your savings account in case an emergency occurs. And, of course, it will! That's just life. Kids get sick or hurt, the car needs work, or the oven goes on the fritz. (If you're a renter, you don't need to worry about the oven problem, of course.)

So, what's the right amount to keep in your emergency fund, and where should it live?

Different financial experts in the United States have different opinions regarding the right amount. I've heard ranges anywhere from three months of your monthly expenses, all the way up to nine months. Now, please notice that I said, "monthly expenses," and not "monthly income." Your expenses each month should be less than your income.

Refer to your written budget to determine what your monthly expenses are, as you calculate the amount of money that should be in your emergency fund. You'll need to include your rent or mortgage payment, utility bills, car payment, etc. Anything that you need to pay every month.

As a single parent I understand that it may be difficult to amass an emergency fund that consists of nine months' worth of your expenses. That amount sounds overwhelming! So, there's nothing wrong with sticking a little closer to the low end of the range that is recommended by money experts.

I understand that saving even that amount can sound daunting. Three to six months of expenses is easily several thousand dollars. You may be thinking that you would have to cut back on so many things! But remember, just like we said earlier, having the peace of mind of knowing that there is money in the bank is so much more fulfilling than cable TV or a new purse could ever be.

I remember talking to Dan about saving for emergencies. He worked in the tech industry and earned a good salary. He had even set up automatic payments to be transferred from his checking account to his savings account, so he didn't have to think about it. "Pay yourself first," was Dan's motto.

The problem was that Dan didn't quite understand the purpose of the emergency fund. While he was very good at saving money, he was also good at spending it. As soon as the emergency fund had grown to two or three thousand dollars, he decided it was time to purchase a new piece of stereo equipment, or take a weekend trip.

So, when the water heater needed to be replaced the emergency fund had already been spent on speakers. He needs to rethink the purpose of an emergency fund.

What Is an Emergency?

The goal is to have three to six months of your EXPENSES (not income) saved for emergencies.

The "Beginner" Emergency Fund can be started with $1,000. This amount was selected because most home, medical, or automotive emergencies can be fixed with $1,000.

What is and isn't an emergency?

☐ Stitches

☐ New Car Battery

☐ Christmas

☐ Tickets to Visit Family

☐ Vet Bills

☐ Broken Eyeglasses

☐ Your Daughter Needs to Buy Supplies for a Project that's Due Tomorrow

☐ Killer Sale at Dillard's

☐ Lunch

☐ Kids' Birthday Gifts and Parties

☐ Your Sister Asks to Borrow Money

☐

Retirement

Retirement is something for old people to worry about. If you're a single parent in your twenties or thirties, retirement seems very, very far away. Most people don't retire until they're at least 60 years old; maybe even closer to 70. Why worry about it now?

The key to having a happy, stress-free retirement is starting to save when you are young and working a full-time job.

So many single parents I talk to can't even think about saving for retirement.

David told me, "I have enough headaches making sure that I can buy food every week, and put clothes on their backs. I'm trying to put some money away for their college education; that leaves no money left for my own retirement."

David brought up an excellent point regarding the priorities of saving for your kids' college, versus saving for your own retirement.

Most parents believe that it's more important to save for college. We all put our children's needs before our own, right? That's what we've always done as parents. But we don't always understand that making sure we are saving enough money to retire comfortably is a big part of putting our children first.

Here's what I mean by that. I know that it's completely my responsibility to make sure I have enough money to take care of myself when I retire. I'm not depending on Social Security to take care of me. I'm not even sure it'll be around when I'm ready to retire. I also don't expect my children to have to care for me. That's the last thing I want.

When my children are adults and have families of their own, they'll be busy with their lives. They'll need to care for their children. I don't want my kids to be the lunch meat and cheese stuck between the two pieces of bread that are their own kids and me. You've heard of the "sandwich generation," right? Those are adult children who need to care for their kids and their parents. It happens often. But, if you plan and save properly, you won't need to put your children in that tough situation.

It's so difficult to see that far ahead, when you're still young, and caring for young children. I urge you to think about the future; for you and your kids.

Many employers offer their employees the ability to save a small percentage of their pay. They automatically deduct this amount, so you don't even need to think about it. Additionally, in a 401K plan employers often contribute to the employees' retirement accounts. This is an excellent perk that all employees should take advantage of.

What Does Retirement Look Like?

Ah…..retirement! That magical time in the distant future when you don't have to do anything but sit on the couch all day, or maybe go fishing. The stereotype for retired people is that they spend all of their time going fishing and playing golf. Personally, I'm not a big fan of either.

Many retired people today are working a fun part-time job; and I don't mean being the greeter at a Walmart. (Not that there's anything wrong with that.)

This is the time when you can work for fun, and not because you have to. How much fun would it be to spend a few hours each week working in a book store or gift shop? I know a gentleman who is happily retired, but works for his favorite men's clothing store on the weekends. Can you say employee discount?

There are many advantages to staying busy as you grow older. Working at a job that you really enjoy instills you with a sense of purpose and gives you the opportunity to interact with new people.

I know another woman who was a stay-at-home mom for most of her life. She got her first full-time job when she turned 50, as the office manager at her church. Now, fifteen years later, she runs the place and has no plans of slowing down.

Retirement is also the perfect time to start your own small business. Have you always wanted to make cakes for a living, or sell that awesome BBQ brisket that everyone is always raving about? This is your chance.

Keeping busy as you grow older helps keep you young, healthy, and it could contribute to your retirement savings.

How to Start Saving for Retirement

The best way to start saving for retirement is by using your employer's 401K program, as we mentioned previously. A 401K automatically deducts the amount of money you want to contribute from each paycheck and deposits that money into a retirement account. Many employers will match that amount of money up to a certain percent.

You'll need to find out how much your employer match is. Some employers match up to 3% of your annual salary, some 5%, and with others it's something different. Find out what the match is.

As a young single parent who wants to start saving for retirement, but who doesn't want to miss out on too much of that paycheck, the majority of financial experts recommend contributing the same amount as the employer match. That way, you'll still have the majority of your paycheck to live on, but you'll be taking advantage of that all-important employer match. It is free money, after all.

There are two different types of 401K accounts that your employer may provide. These are:

- Traditional 401K
- Roth 401K

When you make a contribution to a Traditional 401K, the money is taken out of your paycheck before state and federal taxes are taken out. This means that you will have more money left in your paycheck. The money in the Traditional 401K account will grow tax-deferred. This means that you don't pay taxes on the money as it grows; you pay taxes when you take out the money to use in your retirement.

When you contribute to a Roth 401K, the money is deducted from your paycheck after the taxes are taken out. You'll have a little less money in your paycheck, but the Roth 401K offers one significant benefit. When you are ready to retire, you do not pay taxes on money that is withdrawn from the Roth account. That's because you already paid those taxes on that money, *before* you made the contribution.

If your employer offers the Roth 401K option, I recommend that you take advantage of it. The benefit of not paying taxes on the growth when you withdraw the money at retirement far outweighs the post-tax contribution that you are making.

If your employer does not offer the Roth option, then go ahead and sign up for the Traditional 401K. You are still saving for retirement early, giving it the opportunity to grow over time, and you're taking advantage of the employer match. The money is still growing tax deferred, which is an excellent benefit.

If You Don't Have a 401K Plan at Work

Of course, there are many jobs that don't offer a 401K plan. If that's the case for you, it's still possible (and important) to save for retirement. You'll need to open an Individual Retirement Account, or IRA, with a brokerage firm.

There are many different options, so do a little bit of research online, or you could talk to a financial advisor. You should be able to open an IRA with a small initial investment of $50 or $100.

Withdrawing Retirement Funds

The IRS has strict guidelines about how and when you can withdraw money that is in a retirement account. I recommend that you research these rules for the specific retirement account you are investing your money into. Generally, you cannot withdraw money from these accounts until you are a certain age. If you do there are consequences, such as penalty payments.

I urge you not to withdraw money from your retirement accounts early. Don't even borrow the money, unless you are in a dire financial situation.

In the past, I've heard people rationalize their actions when they borrow from their retirement funds. "I'm paying myself back, so it's okay!" is what I often hear. But, why be in debt to yourself? By "borrowing" money from retirement you're missing out on all of the compound interest you would be earning if you had left the money alone.

If you need to stop making contributions for a while due to life circumstances, you should do that before either borrowing or withdrawing money.

Changing Jobs

My father was born in 1932; he never left a job voluntarily in his whole life. That generation believed that you worked for one employer for 30 or 40 years, then you retired. I remember being in high school when he went through a layoff. Dad was devastated. Having to look for a new job was one of the hardest things he had ever done. He had been counting on the theory that if he were loyal to his employer, then his employer would be loyal to him. Unfortunately, it doesn't always work like that.

So if you change jobs for any reason, you'll need to decide what to do with the 401K from your previous employer. Here are your options:

Leave it where it is.

There won't be any financial penalties if you leave your 401K with your previous employer, but it isn't the best option. It isn't uncommon to have multiple jobs within a ten-year period. Let's just say that in ten years, you have three different jobs. If you contribute to a 401K with each of these employers, you'll have accounts in three different locations. It's just messy!

Cash it out

Please, do NOT cash out your 401K! As we discussed earlier, you'll be taxed and penalized. You could lose close to half of the money you've invested.

Roll it over to an Individual Retirement Account (IRA)

This option is the best one. You'll need to open an IRA, either Roth or Traditional, and have your 401K "rolled over" into the 401K. But there's something very important you need to remember; do NOT have the 401K check from your old employer sent directly to you. The IRS will view this as a distribution paid directly to you, and then they'll ding you for taxes and penalties. You'll need to have the check from the 401K funds sent directly to the new IRA account.

It's very common to change jobs from time to time. Make sure that when you leave a company your money leaves too, and you know where it goes!

Action Plan

- Start saving as early as possible.
- Contribute at least up to the employer match.
- If you don't have a 401K plan at work, open an IRA.
- NEVER withdraw money from your retirement account early.
- Don't borrow from retirement unless you are in a dire financial situation.

Quick List—Retirement Tips You Need to Know

401K and IRA plans have different contribution limits.

If you change jobs, you need to roll your 401K over to an IRA.

_____

_____

_____

_____

Traditional IRAs and 401Ks Grow Tax Deferred—Contributions are Pre-Tax

_____

_____

_____

_____

Roth IRAs and 401Ks Grow Tax Free—Contributions are Post-Tax

_____

_____

_____

Sending Your Kids to College Without Racking Up a Mountain of Debt

Sharon and I met several years ago, when we were working together on a Back-to-School Backpack Giveaway event. Her non-profit organization had collected a ton of backpacks, notebooks, markers, colored pencils, even boxes of tissues and tennis shoes, for single parent families. It was a great event, and we served many families that day.

Of course, Sharon and I started talking about money, and what some methods are for single parents to win with money. At that time, Sharon and I were both single moms. She told me that she had recently moved from New Mexico, where her daughter could have had free tuition at an in-state university. This scholarship is offered to New Mexico high school students who maintain a high GPA throughout their high school career, along with several other requirements.

I thought this sounded great. Who wouldn't want to take advantage of this kind of program? Well, it turned out that Sharon's daughter didn't want to. She had it in her head that she needed to attend a university in another state. As we all know, out-of-state tuition is typically astronomical. This young girl who had the opportunity to attend college in her home state for FREE, told Sharon that it would better for her to go to a different university, where the tuition costs were approximately $20,000 per year. And Sharon agreed!

As we continued to talk, Sharon told me that she had taken out a Parent PLUS loan for her daughter. This is a federal student loan that parents take out on behalf of their children, to pay for their college education. Sharon had borrowed $50,000 to send her daughter to college. It was an investment in her child's future, right? Wrong!

Sharon's daughter dropped out of college, and left her mother footing this enormous bill. According to CollegeAtlas.org, less than two-thirds of college students actually graduate. Thirty percent of freshmen drop out after their first year. But so many people, just like Sharon, are stuck paying back that loan even though they do not have a degree.

It is a terrible misconception in this country that in order to go to college and get a degree, you must take out thousands of dollars in student loans. Banks will tell you that you don't have to make any payments while you're in school, which is true. They just forget to inform students of the crushing debt that will be waiting for them when they finish school, either with or without that degree.

So, as single parents what can you do to help your child get a college education without taking out student loans? I'm glad you asked! There are many things you can do, depending upon the age of your kiddo, that will help.

College Savings Account

If you still have little ones, it's a great idea to open a college savings account as early as possible. The most commonly used account is called a 529 Plan. That just means that it's in section 529 of the Internal Revenue Code. The beautiful advantage about this plan is that the money in the account grows tax free, as long as it ends up being used for educational expenses. You would typically open a college savings account with a brokerage company such as Vanguard, and select investments such as mutual funds.

Don't let that scare you. It is not difficult to go online to Vanguard.com and click the "Open an Account" button. You can start with as little as just a few hundred dollars.

Wait a minute - "As little as? What does she mean, 'As little as?' A few hundred dollars is a lot of money, and I can't open a college account if that's what it takes!"

I get that; I really do! While a brokerage company might not think that's a large amount of money, I certainly do, and I'm sure that you do. It's okay to start small; at least you're starting.

It's perfectly fine to open a savings account with your local bank or credit union, and call that the "college fund" until you have enough money to open that 529 plan. Do your best to budget $5 or $10 every week to deposit into the college fund.

Of course, I like the idea of asking family members to contribute to the cause. When your kiddo's birthday rolls around, see if Grandma can put a little bit into that account. Every little bit will help and before you know it, you'll have what you need. As a grandma myself, I love doing things for the grandkids. I opened savings accounts for both of them when they were babies, and every time I get paid, they each get $10. It's not a huge amount, but over time it certainly adds up.

Setting up an automatic transfer from your checking account to the savings account will help ensure that you consistently help that fund grow.

You might ask, "What if my child ends up getting a full scholarship, or not going to college at all?" These are great questions, and these situations certainly are possible. First, if your kiddo is lucky enough to earn an academic or athletic scholarship that will pay for all college expenses, then you can assign a different family member as the beneficiary of the fund. If you have another child who can use the money, that's great! If not, then you could use it for yourself! Isn't that awesome?

Note: That part is only true as long as the beneficiary does not have to be under a certain age. Double check that requirement when you open your account!

What if your child decides that college is not the right solution for him or her? That's okay! There are so many other educational and career options available. A four-year university education is not the answer for everyone. The money in the college fund can be used to pay for trade schools, as well. Your child might be interested in becoming a welder, electrician, or a hair stylist. These are all wonderful career options, and there are many fine institutions where your child can learn one of these trades.

Dual-Credit Classes

I first learned about dual-credit classes when my daughter was starting high school. This is an excellent program offered in many schools that provide an opportunity for high school students to earn college credit while they are still attending high school. Kids can take classes that count toward both high school graduation AND college!

High schools around the country are partnering with community colleges in their area to provide this service. In most cases, students don't need to leave their high school campus in order to take the classes. Each school district has different guidelines for their own dual-credit programs. I know that in our district, students were not able to take these classes until they were juniors in high school. So, registration began when they were sophomores. There was a fee to take the classes, and they needed to start with U.S. History, Government, or Economics. The fee was minimal; nothing like the cost of university classes.

If kids took all available classes through this program in my local school district, they would have been able to graduate from high school with one year's worth of college credit. The potential to save money this way is enormous.

All school districts have different guidelines, so make sure you check with yours. A different district in my state (Texas) allows students to begin taking dual-credit classes when they are freshmen in high school, and all of the classes are FREE. These students have the amazing opportunity to graduate high school with an Associate's Degree.

Of course, your child will need to have a good understanding of whether or not they want to dedicate themselves to earning a college education. They'll need to be dedicated to taking college level courses, which may be a bit challenging. But with the proper motivation and loving encouragement from you, they will certainly succeed!

Check with your students' counselor to get all the information you need.

Private Scholarships

When people hear the word "scholarship" they immediately think of a full-ride scholarship offered by a university because their student is an exceptional athlete, or because their grade point average is astronomical. While these scholarships are awarded to stellar athletes and students, there IS hope for your average, hard-working, A and B earning student.

There are many organizations, both non-profit and corporations, that offer scholarships to various institutions of higher-learning.

For example, did you know that Duck ® brand duct tape holds a scholarship contest every year for the best prom ensemble made from their products? Do yourself a favor and Google "duct tape scholarship" to see some amazing prom creations.

Now, these private scholarships are not "full rides." The trick is that your hard-working, motivated child needs to research opportunities that are available, both locally and online. It isn't enough to apply for one or two scholarships that they find. They'll need to apply for many; perhaps all the scholarships they qualify for. This means they'll probably be writing many, many essays.

Some private scholarships, such as the Duck ® brand contest, do not involve writing an essay, but most of them do. Again, it depends on how committed your son or daughter is to going to college. It's important that you, as their parent, teach them that borrowing a boat-load of money for school is not how it's going to be done. Model to them how being debt-free is the right way to live. Don't even discuss it as an option.

Unfortunately, you may run into some resistance from the counselors at the high school who discuss "financial-aid" options with your student. Instead of "financial-aid" they are often talking about student loans!

Do your homework when it comes to private scholarships. One great resource is www.FastWeb.com. This website lists thousands of scholarships. I highly recommend that you register on FastWeb, if you're looking for help paying for your child's higher education.

Of course, your child will need to take the initiative to search for and apply for the scholarships. You can't do it for them. The conversation between you and your child about how college will be paid for must happen early and often. Don't wait until their junior year in high school to discuss plans for the future. Honestly, middle school is not too early.

I certainly don't expect a 13-year-old to know what they want to do for the rest of their lives, but it's appropriate to start talking about college. Be very clear that student loans will not be used to pay for the bulk of their education. They also need to understand that they're going to have some skin in the game. Paying for school is not all on you. Make sure they understand what the options are, including dual-credit classes and private scholarships. Visit the school counselor together, so you both understand what is available in your district.

Should All Kids Go to College?

There is another myth in this country that in order to be a success, you must have a college degree. The only way your child is going to get a good job that pays a decent salary is to go to college. While earning a degree is certainly an admirable accomplishment, it isn't necessarily the best path for everyone.

Americans seem to have forgotten that there are many trades that don't require a degree. Do you remember this joke?

A prominent lawyer calls a plumber to fix a leak in his shower. After about 25 minutes the plumber hands him a bill for $200.00. The lawyer, enraged, says: "I'm a famous trial lawyer, and even I don't make that kind of money for 25 minutes work!" "Neither did I when I was a lawyer," says the plumber.

Many of the so-called "blue collar" jobs offer excellent salaries and benefits. And, did you know that they frequently offer on-the-job training? This is specific to each individual company, so make sure you check with them.

I recently noticed a local electrical company that had signs in front of their building for months that read, "Hiring—Entry Level—Will Train." What an excellent opportunity for a young person who isn't interested in going to college.

Now, you may be thinking, "That's fine for my son, but what about my daughter?" I see no problem whatsoever in young women learning the same kind of trade skills as young men.

So, which jobs are included in these trades?

- Electrician
- Plumber
- Mechanic
- Welder

- Heating and Air Conditioning
- Construction

Any one of these jobs can become a lifelong career, or even transformed into a small business. I recently had some plumbing work completed at my house; a toilet needed to be replaced. The plumber who did the job was a retired police officer. He said he started this business because he loved it. Maybe your child would love plumbing, or maybe they wouldn't—but don't be afraid to research the options for a great career that don't require a college degree.

If your child is interested in pursuing a trade, be sure to look into Mike Rowe's foundation. He offers a wealth of information regarding the skills gap and the growing need for skilled trades-people.

There's a shortage of young people who see the value of learning a trade instead of going to college. It has been drilled into our children's heads (and ours) that in order to be successful in this country, it's mandatory to have a college degree. This isn't true.

Your child can have a successful career with or without a degree. If they do choose to go to college, make sure they explore all options to help them avoid crushing student loan debt.

Action Plan

- Talk to your kids about college. Find out if it's best for them to go to college right out of high school.
- If college is the right path, have them start attending dual-credit classes at their high school as soon as possible.
- Look into your local community college. Your kiddo should get their first two years out of the way there.
- Point your kiddo in the direction of private scholarships (like FastWeb.com).

100-Day Action Plan

It takes about 90 days, or three months, to really get a handle on your budget. Use this Action Plan to write down EVERYTHING.

During the first month, you'll want to accomplish the following tasks:

- Let your children know about your new plan. It's important that you include them. Remember, it's our job as parents to teach our kids how to manage money.
- Gather all of your bills together and determine when everything is due. Log into your bank to see auto-pay dates and payment amounts. Write it all down.
- Plug these due dates and amounts into a budget app or worksheets.
- Start building your envelope system. Think about the categories you'll need for each one. Label each envelope with a category.
- Create your budget using either an app, pen and paper, or by creating the sheets on your computer. It's all up to you! Remember to take your pay schedule into account. Do you get paid weekly, every other week, or semi-monthly? Make sure to note which bills come out of each paycheck.
- Find out how much debt you have. Write it all down.
- If you're not contributing to your company's 401K program, begin contributing up to the employer match.

THIS WEEK'S GOALS

Starts _____/_____/_____   **Ends** _____/_____/_____

Top Three

1

2

3

Figure out how much you owe. Gather all of your debts and come up with a total. Also note the due dates for the payments.

Other Goals

In the beginning of this journey, it's a great idea to sit down with your kids and tell them about your plan. Explain to them about how you'll all be on a budget and how the envelope system works. Be positive – let them know that being intentional with money will help all of you.

DAY 1

MONDAY /

Top Three Tasks

1

2

3

Other Tasks

Schedule

7 AM

8 AM

9 AM

10 AM

11 AM

12 PM

1 PM

2 PM

3 PM

4 PM

5 PM

6 PM

7 PM

8 PM

9 PM

10 PM

DAY 2

TUESDAY _____ / ____

Top Three Tasks

1 _____
2 _____
3 _____

Other Tasks

_____
_____
_____
_____
_____
_____
_____
_____
_____
_____
_____
_____
_____
_____

Schedule

7 AM _____
8 AM _____
9 AM _____
10 AM _____
11 AM _____
12 PM _____
1 PM _____
2 PM _____
3 PM _____
4 PM _____
5 PM _____
6 PM _____
7 PM _____
8 PM _____
9 PM _____
10 PM _____

SHOW YOUR PAYCHECK WHO'S BOSS!

WEDNESDAY

DAY 3

Top Three Tasks

1 ....

2 ....

3 ....

Other Tasks

....
....
....
....
....
....
....
....
....
....
....
....
....
....
....
....
....

Schedule

7 AM ....

8 AM ....

9 AM ....

10 AM ....

11 AM ....

12 PM ....

1 PM ....

2 PM ....

3 PM ....

4 PM ....

5 PM ....

6 PM ....

7 PM ....

8 PM ....

9 PM ....

10 PM ....

DAY 4

THURSDAY _____ / _____

Top Three Tasks

1 _____

2 _____

3 _____

_____

Other Tasks

_____
_____
_____
_____
_____
_____
_____
_____
_____
_____
_____
_____
_____
_____

Schedule

7 AM
8 AM
9 AM
10 AM
11 AM
12 PM
1 PM
2 PM
3 PM
4 PM
5 PM
6 PM
7 PM
8 PM
9 PM
10 PM

SHOW YOUR PAYCHECK WHO'S BOSS!

 FRIDAY

DAY 5

Top Three Tasks

1

2

3

Other Tasks

Schedule

7 AM

8 AM

9 AM

10 AM

11 AM

12 PM

1 PM

2 PM

3 PM

4 PM

5 PM

6 PM

7 PM

8 PM

9 PM

10 PM

DAY 6

Top Three Tasks

1 _____

2 _____

3 _____

_____

Other Tasks

_____
_____
_____
_____
_____
_____
_____
_____
_____
_____
_____
_____
_____
_____
_____
_____

Schedule

7 AM _____

8 AM _____

9 AM _____

10 AM _____

11 AM _____

12 PM _____

1 PM _____

2 PM _____

3 PM _____

4 PM _____

5 PM _____

6 PM _____

7 PM _____

8 PM _____

9 PM _____

10 PM _____

SHOW YOUR PAYCHECK WHO'S BOSS!

DAY 7

SUNDAY

Top Three Tasks

1 ....

2 ....

3 ....

Other Tasks

....

....

....

....

....

....

....

....

....

....

....

....

....

....

....

Schedule

7 AM ....

8 AM ....

9 AM ....

10 AM ....

11 AM ....

12 PM ....

1 PM ....

2 PM ....

3 PM ....

4 PM ....

5 PM ....

6 PM ....

7 PM ....

8 PM ....

9 PM ....

10 PM ....

THIS WEEK'S GOALS

Starts _____ / _____   **Ends** _____ / _____

Top Three

①
②   Figure out EXACTLY when all of your monthly bills are due. Which day of the month, and the amount of each payment.
③

Other Goals

_____
_____
_____
_____
_____
_____
_____
_____
_____
_____
_____
_____
_____
_____

DAY 8

MONDAY

Top Three Tasks

1

2

3

Other Tasks

Schedule

7 AM

8 AM

9 AM

10 AM

11 AM

12 PM

1 PM

2 PM

3 PM

4 PM

5 PM

6 PM

7 PM

8 PM

9 PM

10 PM

DAY 9

TUESDAY _____ / _____

Top Three Tasks

1 _____

2 _____

3 _____

Other Tasks

_____
_____
_____
_____
_____
_____
_____
_____
_____
_____
_____
_____
_____
_____
_____

Schedule

7 AM _____

8 AM _____

9 AM _____

10 AM _____

11 AM _____

12 PM _____

1 PM _____

2 PM _____

3 PM _____

4 PM _____

5 PM _____

6 PM _____

7 PM _____

8 PM _____

9 PM _____

10 PM _____

DAY 10

WEDNESDAY

Top Three Tasks

1 ....

2 ....

3 ....

Other Tasks

....

....

....

....

....

....

....

....

....

....

....

....

Schedule

7 AM ....

8 AM ....

9 AM ....

10 AM ....

11 AM ....

12 PM ....

1 PM ....

2 PM ....

3 PM ....

4 PM ....

5 PM ....

6 PM ....

7 PM ....

8 PM ....

9 PM ....

10 PM ....

DAY 11

Top Three Tasks

1 ....

2 ....

3 ....

Other Tasks

Schedule

7 AM

8 AM

9 AM

10 AM

11 AM

12 PM

1 PM

2 PM

3 PM

4 PM

5 PM

6 PM

7 PM

8 PM

9 PM

10 PM

DAY 12

/ / FRIDAY

Top Three Tasks

1 ....

2 ....

3 ....

Other Tasks

Schedule

7 AM ....

8 AM ....

9 AM ....

10 AM ....

11 AM ....

12 PM ....

1 PM ....

2 PM ....

3 PM ....

4 PM ....

5 PM ....

6 PM ....

7 PM ....

8 PM ....

9 PM ....

10 PM ....

DAY 13

SATURDAY _____ / ____

Top Three Tasks

1. _____
2. _____
3. _____

Other Tasks

_____
_____
_____
_____
_____
_____
_____
_____
_____
_____
_____
_____
_____
_____

Schedule

7 AM
8 AM
9 AM
10 AM
11 AM
12 PM
1 PM
2 PM
3 PM
4 PM
5 PM
6 PM
7 PM
8 PM
9 PM
10 PM

DAY 14

SUNDAY

Top Three Tasks

1 ....

2 ....

3 ....

Other Tasks

....

....

....

....

....

....

....

....

....

....

....

....

....

Schedule

7 AM ....

8 AM ....

9 AM ....

10 AM ....

11 AM ....

12 PM ....

1 PM ....

2 PM ....

3 PM ....

4 PM ....

5 PM ....

6 PM ....

7 PM ....

8 PM ....

9 PM ....

10 PM ....

THIS WEEK'S GOALS

Starts _____/_____   **Ends** _____/_____

Top Three

①

② Are you still working on all of those due dates? That's okay – it can take some time.

③

Other Goals

_____
_____
_____
_____
_____
_____
_____
_____
_____
_____
_____
_____

SHOW YOUR PAYCHECK WHO'S BOSS!

MONDAY

DAY 15

Top Three Tasks

1

2

3

Other Tasks

Schedule

7 AM

8 AM

9 AM

10 AM

11 AM

12 PM

1 PM

2 PM

3 PM

4 PM

5 PM

6 PM

7 PM

8 PM

9 PM

10 PM

DAY 16

TUESDAY

Top Three Tasks

1

2

3

Other Tasks

Schedule

7 AM

8 AM

9 AM

10 AM

11 AM

12 PM

1 PM

2 PM

3 PM

4 PM

5 PM

6 PM

7 PM

8 PM

9 PM

10 PM

SHOW YOUR PAYCHECK WHO'S BOSS!

WEDNESDAY

DAY 17

Top Three Tasks

1
2
3

Other Tasks

Schedule

7 AM
8 AM
9 AM
10 AM
11 AM
12 PM
1 PM
2 PM
3 PM
4 PM
5 PM
6 PM
7 PM
8 PM
9 PM
10 PM

DAY 18

Top Three Tasks

1 _____

2 _____

3 _____

Other Tasks

_____
_____
_____
_____
_____
_____
_____
_____
_____
_____
_____
_____
_____
_____
_____
_____

Schedule

7 AM _____
8 AM _____
9 AM _____
10 AM _____
11 AM _____
12 PM _____
1 PM _____
2 PM _____
3 PM _____
4 PM _____
5 PM _____
6 PM _____
7 PM _____
8 PM _____
9 PM _____
10 PM _____

DAY 19

FRIDAY /

Top Three Tasks

1 ....

2 ....

3 ....

Other Tasks

....
....
....
....
....
....
....
....
....
....
....
....
....
....
....

Schedule

7 AM
8 AM
9 AM
10 AM
11 AM
12 PM
1 PM
2 PM
3 PM
4 PM
5 PM
6 PM
7 PM
8 PM
9 PM
10 PM

DAY 20

SATURDAY _____ / ____

Top Three Tasks

1 _____

2 _____

3 _____
_____

Other Tasks

_____
_____
_____
_____
_____
_____
_____
_____
_____
_____
_____
_____
_____
_____
_____

Schedule

7 AM
8 AM
9 AM
10 AM
11 AM
12 PM
1 PM
2 PM
3 PM
4 PM
5 PM
6 PM
7 PM
8 PM
9 PM
10 PM

DAY 21

SUNDAY

Top Three Tasks

1
2
3

Other Tasks

Schedule

7 AM
8 AM
9 AM
10 AM
11 AM
12 PM
1 PM
2 PM
3 PM
4 PM
5 PM
6 PM
7 PM
8 PM
9 PM
10 PM

THIS WEEK'S GOALS

Starts _____ **Ends** _____

Top Three

1.

2.

3.

> Now that you know when your bills are due, figure out which paycheck those payments will come out of. This shouldn't take too long.

Other Goals

_____

_____

_____

_____

_____

_____

_____

_____

_____

_____

_____

_____

_____

_____

_____

_____

_____ / _____ MONDAY

DAY 22

Top Three Tasks

1 ....

2 ....

3 ....

Other Tasks

Schedule

7 AM

8 AM

9 AM

10 AM

11 AM

12 PM

1 PM

2 PM

3 PM

4 PM

5 PM

6 PM

7 PM

8 PM

9 PM

10 PM

DAY 23

TUESDAY _____ / ____

Top Three Tasks

1 _____

2 _____

3 _____

Other Tasks

_____
_____
_____
_____
_____
_____
_____
_____
_____
_____
_____
_____
_____
_____
_____
_____

Schedule

7 AM _____
8 AM _____
9 AM _____
10 AM _____
11 AM _____
12 PM _____
1 PM _____
2 PM _____
3 PM _____
4 PM _____
5 PM _____
6 PM _____
7 PM _____
8 PM _____
9 PM _____
10 PM _____

WEDNESDAY

DAY 24

Top Three Tasks

1 _____

2 _____

3 _____

Other Tasks

_____
_____
_____
_____
_____
_____
_____
_____
_____
_____
_____
_____
_____
_____
_____

Schedule

7 AM _____

8 AM _____

9 AM _____

10 AM _____

11 AM _____

12 PM _____

1 PM _____

2 PM _____

3 PM _____

4 PM _____

5 PM _____

6 PM _____

7 PM _____

8 PM _____

9 PM _____

10 PM _____

DAY 25

Top Three Tasks

1
2
3

Other Tasks

Schedule

7 AM
8 AM
9 AM
10 AM
11 AM
12 PM
1 PM
2 PM
3 PM
4 PM
5 PM
6 PM
7 PM
8 PM
9 PM
10 PM

DAY 26

Top Three Tasks	Schedule
1 _____	7 AM _____
2 _____	8 AM _____
3 _____	9 AM _____
	10 AM _____
Other Tasks	11 AM _____
	12 PM _____
	1 PM _____
	2 PM _____
	3 PM _____
	4 PM _____
	5 PM _____
	6 PM _____
	7 PM _____
	8 PM _____
	9 PM _____
	10 PM _____

FRIDAY

DAY 27

SATURDAY _____ / _____

Top Three Tasks

1 _____

2 _____

3 _____

_____

Other Tasks

_____
_____
_____
_____
_____
_____
_____
_____
_____
_____
_____
_____
_____
_____

Schedule

7 AM
8 AM
9 AM
10 AM
11 AM
12 PM
1 PM
2 PM
3 PM
4 PM
5 PM
6 PM
7 PM
8 PM
9 PM
10 PM

SHOW YOUR PAYCHECK WHO'S BOSS!

SUNDAY

DAY 28

Top Three Tasks

Schedule

1

2

3

Other Tasks

7 AM
8 AM
9 AM
10 AM
11 AM
12 PM
1 PM
2 PM
3 PM
4 PM
5 PM
6 PM
7 PM
8 PM
9 PM
10 PM

THIS WEEK'S GOALS

Starts _____ **Ends** _____

Top Three

① Start creating your budget, whether it's
② electronic or on paper. Enter your pay
dates and the dates you need to pay bills.
③

Other Goals

_____
_____
_____
_____
_____
_____
_____
_____
_____
_____
_____
_____
_____
_____

SHOW YOUR PAYCHECK WHO'S BOSS!

MONDAY

DAY 29

Top Three Tasks

1

2

3

Other Tasks

Schedule

7 AM

8 AM

9 AM

10 AM

11 AM

12 PM

1 PM

2 PM

3 PM

4 PM

5 PM

6 PM

7 PM

8 PM

9 PM

10 PM

DAY 30

TUESDAY _____ / _____

Top Three Tasks

1 _____

2 _____

3 _____

Other Tasks

_____
_____
_____
_____
_____
_____
_____
_____
_____
_____
_____
_____
_____
_____

Schedule

7 AM _____
8 AM _____
9 AM _____
10 AM _____
11 AM _____
12 PM _____
1 PM _____
2 PM _____
3 PM _____
4 PM _____
5 PM _____
6 PM _____
7 PM _____
8 PM _____
9 PM _____
10 PM _____

WEDNESDAY

DAY 31

Top Three Tasks

1
2
3

Other Tasks

Schedule

7 AM
8 AM
9 AM
10 AM
11 AM
12 PM
1 PM
2 PM
3 PM
4 PM
5 PM
6 PM
7 PM
8 PM
9 PM
10 PM

DAY 32

THURSDAY   /

Top Three Tasks

1
2
3

Other Tasks

Schedule

7 AM
8 AM
9 AM
10 AM
11 AM
12 PM
1 PM
2 PM
3 PM
4 PM
5 PM
6 PM
7 PM
8 PM
9 PM
10 PM

DAY 33

FRIDAY

Top Three Tasks

1 _____

2 _____

3 _____

Other Tasks

_____
_____
_____
_____
_____
_____
_____
_____
_____
_____
_____
_____
_____
_____
_____
_____
_____

Schedule

7 AM
8 AM
9 AM
10 AM
11 AM
12 PM
1 PM
2 PM
3 PM
4 PM
5 PM
6 PM
7 PM
8 PM
9 PM
10 PM

DAY 34

Top Three Tasks

1 _____

2 _____

3 _____

Other Tasks

_____
_____
_____
_____
_____
_____
_____
_____
_____
_____
_____
_____
_____
_____
_____
_____

Schedule

7 AM
8 AM
9 AM
10 AM
11 AM
12 PM
1 PM
2 PM
3 PM
4 PM
5 PM
6 PM
7 PM
8 PM
9 PM
10 PM

SUNDAY

DAY
35

Top Three Tasks

1
2
3

Other Tasks

Schedule

7 AM
8 AM
9 AM
10 AM
11 AM
12 PM
1 PM
2 PM
3 PM
4 PM
5 PM
6 PM
7 PM
8 PM
9 PM
10 PM

THIS WEEK'S GOALS

Starts _____/_____/_____   **Ends** _____/_____/_____

Top Three

① ②
③

Create your envelopes! Involve your kids in this exercise. It should be fun. Add your envelope categories and amounts to your written budget.

Other Goals

_____
_____
_____
_____
_____
_____
_____
_____
_____
_____
_____
_____
_____
_____
_____

MONDAY

**DAY
36**

Top Three Tasks

1 ....

2 ....

3 ....

....

Other Tasks

Schedule

7 AM ....

8 AM ....

9 AM ....

10 AM ....

11 AM ....

12 PM ....

1 PM ....

2 PM ....

3 PM ....

4 PM ....

5 PM ....

6 PM ....

7 PM ....

8 PM ....

9 PM ....

10 PM ....

DAY 37

TUESDAY _____ / ____

Top Three Tasks

1 _____

2 _____

3 _____

Other Tasks

_____
_____
_____
_____
_____
_____
_____
_____
_____
_____
_____
_____
_____
_____
_____

Schedule

7 AM _____

8 AM _____

9 AM _____

10 AM _____

11 AM _____

12 PM _____

1 PM _____

2 PM _____

3 PM _____

4 PM _____

5 PM _____

6 PM _____

7 PM _____

8 PM _____

9 PM _____

10 PM _____

SHOW YOUR PAYCHECK WHO'S BOSS!

WEDNESDAY

DAY 38

Top Three Tasks

1
2
3

Other Tasks

Schedule

7 AM
8 AM
9 AM
10 AM
11 AM
12 PM
1 PM
2 PM
3 PM
4 PM
5 PM
6 PM
7 PM
8 PM
9 PM
10 PM

DAY 39

Top Three Tasks

1 _____

2 _____

3 _____
_____

Other Tasks

_____
_____
_____
_____
_____
_____
_____
_____
_____
_____
_____
_____
_____
_____
_____
_____
_____

Schedule

7 AM
8 AM
9 AM
10 AM
11 AM
12 PM
1 PM
2 PM
3 PM
4 PM
5 PM
6 PM
7 PM
8 PM
9 PM
10 PM

FRIDAY

**DAY
40**

Top Three Tasks

1

2

3

Other Tasks

Schedule

7 AM

8 AM

9 AM

10 AM

11 AM

12 PM

1 PM

2 PM

3 PM

4 PM

5 PM

6 PM

7 PM

8 PM

9 PM

10 PM

DAY 41

SATURDAY _____ / ___

Top Three Tasks

1 _____

2 _____

3 _____

Other Tasks

_____
_____
_____
_____
_____
_____
_____
_____
_____
_____
_____
_____
_____
_____
_____

Schedule

7 AM
8 AM
9 AM
10 AM
11 AM
12 PM
1 PM
2 PM
3 PM
4 PM
5 PM
6 PM
7 PM
8 PM
9 PM
10 PM

SUNDAY

DAY 42

Top Three Tasks

1 _____

2 _____

3 _____

Other Tasks

_____
_____
_____
_____
_____
_____
_____
_____
_____
_____
_____
_____
_____
_____

Schedule

7 AM _____

8 AM _____

9 AM _____

10 AM _____

11 AM _____

12 PM _____

1 PM _____

2 PM _____

3 PM _____

4 PM _____

5 PM _____

6 PM _____

7 PM _____

8 PM _____

9 PM _____

10 PM _____

THIS WEEK'S GOALS

Starts _____ / _____   **Ends** _____ / _____

Top Three

① ② ③

Work the budget – don't spend money unless you have the cash. Use your envelopes.

Other Goals

As you get ready for each day, think about what you'll need to do. Will you stop at the grocery store after work? Make sure you bring your Groceries envelope with you. Did you promise the kids they have take-out for dinner? Grab the Eating Out envelope before you leave the house.

MONDAY

DAY 43

Top Three Tasks

1

2

3

Other Tasks

Schedule

7 AM

8 AM

9 AM

10 AM

11 AM

12 PM

1 PM

2 PM

3 PM

4 PM

5 PM

6 PM

7 PM

8 PM

9 PM

10 PM

DAY 44

TUESDAY _____ / ____

Top Three Tasks

1 _____

2 _____

3 _____

Other Tasks

_____
_____
_____
_____
_____
_____
_____
_____
_____
_____
_____
_____
_____
_____
_____

Schedule

7 AM _____

8 AM _____

9 AM _____

10 AM _____

11 AM _____

12 PM _____

1 PM _____

2 PM _____

3 PM _____

4 PM _____

5 PM _____

6 PM _____

7 PM _____

8 PM _____

9 PM _____

10 PM _____

DAY 45

WEDNESDAY

Top Three Tasks

1 _____

2 _____

3 _____

Other Tasks

_____
_____
_____
_____
_____
_____
_____
_____
_____
_____
_____
_____

Schedule

7 AM
8 AM
9 AM
10 AM
11 AM
12 PM
1 PM
2 PM
3 PM
4 PM
5 PM
6 PM
7 PM
8 PM
9 PM
10 PM

DAY 46

Top Three Tasks

1
2
3

Other Tasks

Schedule

7 AM
8 AM
9 AM
10 AM
11 AM
12 PM
1 PM
2 PM
3 PM
4 PM
5 PM
6 PM
7 PM
8 PM
9 PM
10 PM

DAY 47

/ FRIDAY

Top Three Tasks

1 ....

2 ....

3 ....

Other Tasks

Schedule

7 AM

8 AM

9 AM

10 AM

11 AM

12 PM

1 PM

2 PM

3 PM

4 PM

5 PM

6 PM

7 PM

8 PM

9 PM

10 PM

DAY 48

SATURDAY _____ / ____

Top Three Tasks

1 _____

2 _____

3 _____

Other Tasks

_____
_____
_____
_____
_____
_____
_____
_____
_____
_____
_____
_____
_____
_____

Schedule

7 AM
8 AM
9 AM
10 AM
11 AM
12 PM
1 PM
2 PM
3 PM
4 PM
5 PM
6 PM
7 PM
8 PM
9 PM
10 PM

DAY 49

SUNDAY

Top Three Tasks

1 _____

2 _____

3 _____

Other Tasks

_____
_____
_____
_____
_____
_____
_____
_____
_____
_____
_____
_____
_____
_____

Schedule

7 AM

8 AM

9 AM

10 AM

11 AM

12 PM

1 PM

2 PM

3 PM

4 PM

5 PM

6 PM

7 PM

8 PM

9 PM

10 PM

THIS WEEK'S GOALS

Starts _____ / _____   **Ends** _____ / _____

Top Three

①

② You're doing great! Keep going!

③

Other Goals

_____
_____
_____
_____
_____
_____
_____
_____
_____
_____
_____
_____
_____
_____

DAY 50

/ MONDAY

Top Three Tasks

1 ....

2 ....

3 ....

Other Tasks

....
....
....
....
....
....
....
....
....
....
....
....
....
....

Schedule

7 AM ....

8 AM ....

9 AM ....

10 AM ....

11 AM ....

12 PM ....

1 PM ....

2 PM ....

3 PM ....

4 PM ....

5 PM ....

6 PM ....

7 PM ....

8 PM ....

9 PM ....

10 PM ....

DAY 51

TUESDAY _____ / ____

Top Three Tasks

1 _____

2 _____

3 _____

Other Tasks

_____
_____
_____
_____
_____
_____
_____
_____
_____
_____
_____
_____
_____
_____
_____

Schedule

7 AM _____

8 AM _____

9 AM _____

10 AM _____

11 AM _____

12 PM _____

1 PM _____

2 PM _____

3 PM _____

4 PM _____

5 PM _____

6 PM _____

7 PM _____

8 PM _____

9 PM _____

10 PM _____

DAY 52

WEDNESDAY

Top Three Tasks

1
2
3

Other Tasks

Schedule

7 AM
8 AM
9 AM
10 AM
11 AM
12 PM
1 PM
2 PM
3 PM
4 PM
5 PM
6 PM
7 PM
8 PM
9 PM
10 PM

DAY 53

THURSDAY _____ / _____

Top Three Tasks

1 _____

2 _____

3 _____

_____

Other Tasks

_____
_____
_____
_____
_____
_____
_____
_____
_____
_____
_____
_____
_____
_____
_____

Schedule

7 AM _____

8 AM _____

9 AM _____

10 AM _____

11 AM _____

12 PM _____

1 PM _____

2 PM _____

3 PM _____

4 PM _____

5 PM _____

6 PM _____

7 PM _____

8 PM _____

9 PM _____

10 PM _____

DAY 54

FRIDAY

Top Three Tasks

1 ....

2 ....

3 ....
....

Other Tasks

Schedule

7 AM

8 AM

9 AM

10 AM

11 AM

12 PM

1 PM

2 PM

3 PM

4 PM

5 PM

6 PM

7 PM

8 PM

9 PM

10 PM

DAY 55

SATURDAY _____ / ____

Top Three Tasks

1 _____

2 _____

3 _____

Other Tasks

_____

_____

_____

_____

_____

_____

_____

_____

_____

_____

_____

_____

_____

_____

_____

_____

Schedule

7 AM

8 AM

9 AM

10 AM

11 AM

12 PM

1 PM

2 PM

3 PM

4 PM

5 PM

6 PM

7 PM

8 PM

9 PM

10 PM

DAY 56

SUNDAY

Top Three Tasks

1
2
3

Other Tasks

Schedule

7 AM
8 AM
9 AM
10 AM
11 AM
12 PM
1 PM
2 PM
3 PM
4 PM
5 PM
6 PM
7 PM
8 PM
9 PM
10 PM

THIS WEEK'S GOALS

Starts _____   **Ends** _____

Top Three

①

②

③

> Are you finding that you need to make some adjustments to your budget? That's fine! This is the time to do it.

Other Goals

_____
_____
_____
_____
_____
_____
_____
_____
_____
_____
_____
_____
_____
_____

DAY 57

MONDAY

Top Three Tasks

1 ....

2 ....

3 ....

Other Tasks

....
....
....
....
....
....
....
....
....
....
....
....
....
....
....

Schedule

7 AM

8 AM

9 AM

10 AM

11 AM

12 PM

1 PM

2 PM

3 PM

4 PM

5 PM

6 PM

7 PM

8 PM

9 PM

10 PM

DAY 58

TUESDAY _____ / ___

Top Three Tasks

1 _____

2 _____

3 _____

_____

Other Tasks

_____

_____

_____

_____

_____

_____

_____

_____

_____

_____

_____

_____

_____

_____

Schedule

7 AM _____

8 AM _____

9 AM _____

10 AM _____

11 AM _____

12 PM _____

1 PM _____

2 PM _____

3 PM _____

4 PM _____

5 PM _____

6 PM _____

7 PM _____

8 PM _____

9 PM _____

10 PM _____

DAY 59

WEDNESDAY

Top Three Tasks

1 ....

2 ....

3 ....

Other Tasks

....

....

....

....

....

....

....

....

....

....

....

....

....

....

Schedule

7 AM ....

8 AM ....

9 AM ....

10 AM ....

11 AM ....

12 PM ....

1 PM ....

2 PM ....

3 PM ....

4 PM ....

5 PM ....

6 PM ....

7 PM ....

8 PM ....

9 PM ....

10 PM ....

DAY 60

THURSDAY   /

Top Three Tasks

1

2

3

Other Tasks

Schedule

7 AM

8 AM

9 AM

10 AM

11 AM

12 PM

1 PM

2 PM

3 PM

4 PM

5 PM

6 PM

7 PM

8 PM

9 PM

10 PM

DAY 61

FRIDAY

Top Three Tasks

1

2

3

Other Tasks

Schedule

7 AM

8 AM

9 AM

10 AM

11 AM

12 PM

1 PM

2 PM

3 PM

4 PM

5 PM

6 PM

7 PM

8 PM

9 PM

10 PM

DAY 62

SATURDAY   /

Top Three Tasks

1 _____

2 _____

3 _____

_____

Other Tasks

_____
_____
_____
_____
_____
_____
_____
_____
_____
_____
_____
_____
_____

Schedule

7 AM
8 AM
9 AM
10 AM
11 AM
12 PM
1 PM
2 PM
3 PM
4 PM
5 PM
6 PM
7 PM
8 PM
9 PM
10 PM

SUNDAY

DAY 63

Top Three Tasks

1 ....

2 ....

3 ....

Other Tasks

....
....
....
....
....
....
....
....
....
....
....
....
....
....
....

Schedule

7 AM

8 AM

9 AM

10 AM

11 AM

12 PM

1 PM

2 PM

3 PM

4 PM

5 PM

6 PM

7 PM

8 PM

9 PM

10 PM

THIS WEEK'S GOALS

Starts _____ / _____   **Ends** _____ / _____

Top Three

(1)

(2)   Review your retirement savings plan.

(3)

Other Goals

DAY 64

Top Three Tasks

1 ....

2 ....

3 ....

Other Tasks

Schedule

7 AM ....

8 AM ....

9 AM ....

10 AM ....

11 AM ....

12 PM ....

1 PM ....

2 PM ....

3 PM ....

4 PM ....

5 PM ....

6 PM ....

7 PM ....

8 PM ....

9 PM ....

10 PM ....

DAY 65

TUESDAY _____ / ____

Top Three Tasks

1 _____

2 _____

3 _____

Other Tasks

_____
_____
_____
_____
_____
_____
_____
_____
_____
_____
_____
_____
_____
_____

Schedule

7 AM _____

8 AM _____

9 AM _____

10 AM _____

11 AM _____

12 PM _____

1 PM _____

2 PM _____

3 PM _____

4 PM _____

5 PM _____

6 PM _____

7 PM _____

8 PM _____

9 PM _____

10 PM _____

WEDNESDAY

DAY 66

Top Three Tasks

1 _____

2 _____

3 _____

Other Tasks

_____
_____
_____
_____
_____
_____
_____
_____
_____
_____
_____
_____
_____
_____

Schedule

7 AM _____
8 AM _____
9 AM _____
10 AM _____
11 AM _____
12 PM _____
1 PM _____
2 PM _____
3 PM _____
4 PM _____
5 PM _____
6 PM _____
7 PM _____
8 PM _____
9 PM _____
10 PM _____

DAY 67

THURSDAY _____ / ____

Top Three Tasks

1 _____

2 _____

3 _____

Other Tasks

_____
_____
_____
_____
_____
_____
_____
_____
_____
_____
_____
_____
_____
_____
_____

Schedule

7 AM _____
8 AM _____
9 AM _____
10 AM _____
11 AM _____
12 PM _____
1 PM _____
2 PM _____
3 PM _____
4 PM _____
5 PM _____
6 PM _____
7 PM _____
8 PM _____
9 PM _____
10 PM _____

SHOW YOUR PAYCHECK WHO'S BOSS!

DAY 68

Top Three Tasks

1

2

3

Other Tasks

Schedule

7 AM

8 AM

9 AM

10 AM

11 AM

12 PM

1 PM

2 PM

3 PM

4 PM

5 PM

6 PM

7 PM

8 PM

9 PM

10 PM

DAY 69

SATURDAY _____ / ____

Top Three Tasks

1 _____
2 _____
3 _____

Other Tasks

_____
_____
_____
_____
_____
_____
_____
_____
_____
_____
_____
_____
_____
_____

Schedule

7 AM _____
8 AM _____
9 AM _____
10 AM _____
11 AM _____
12 PM _____
1 PM _____
2 PM _____
3 PM _____
4 PM _____
5 PM _____
6 PM _____
7 PM _____
8 PM _____
9 PM _____
10 PM _____

SHOW YOUR PAYCHECK WHO'S BOSS!

DAY 70

SUNDAY

Top Three Tasks

1 ....

2 ....

3 ....

Other Tasks

....
....
....
....
....
....
....
....
....
....
....
....
....
....

Schedule

7 AM
8 AM
9 AM
10 AM
11 AM
12 PM
1 PM
2 PM
3 PM
4 PM
5 PM
6 PM
7 PM
8 PM
9 PM
10 PM

THIS WEEK'S GOALS

Starts _____/_____/_____   **Ends** _____/_____/_____

Top Three

①

②

③

At this point, you should have a good handle on your budget, bills, due dates, debts, and all the nuances that are specific to your financial situation.

This is a good time to think about what the hurdles have been. What is proving to be most difficult for you? What is your favorite part of budgeting?

How are your kids responding to this change in lifestyle? Are they fighting you or helping you?

User the remainder of this planner to make notes, or keep track of your financial successes.

You ARE succeeding!

SHOW YOUR PAYCHECK WHO'S BOSS!

DAY 71

MONDAY

Top Three Tasks

1 _____

2 _____

3 _____

Other Tasks

Schedule

7 AM

8 AM

9 AM

10 AM

11 AM

12 PM

1 PM

2 PM

3 PM

4 PM

5 PM

6 PM

7 PM

8 PM

9 PM

10 PM

DAY 72

TUESDAY _____ / _____

Top Three Tasks

1 _____

2 _____

3 _____

Other Tasks

_____
_____
_____
_____
_____
_____
_____
_____
_____
_____
_____
_____
_____
_____
_____
_____
_____

Schedule

7 AM

8 AM

9 AM

10 AM

11 AM

12 PM

1 PM

2 PM

3 PM

4 PM

5 PM

6 PM

7 PM

8 PM

9 PM

10 PM

DAY 73

WEDNESDAY

Top Three Tasks

1 _____

2 _____

3 _____

Other Tasks

_____
_____
_____
_____
_____
_____
_____
_____
_____
_____
_____
_____
_____
_____
_____

Schedule

7 AM _____

8 AM _____

9 AM _____

10 AM _____

11 AM _____

12 PM _____

1 PM _____

2 PM _____

3 PM _____

4 PM _____

5 PM _____

6 PM _____

7 PM _____

8 PM _____

9 PM _____

10 PM _____

DAY 74

THURSDAY _____ / ____

Top Three Tasks

1 _____

2 _____

3 _____
_____

Other Tasks

_____
_____
_____
_____
_____
_____
_____
_____
_____
_____
_____
_____
_____
_____

Schedule

7 AM
8 AM
9 AM
10 AM
11 AM
12 PM
1 PM
2 PM
3 PM
4 PM
5 PM
6 PM
7 PM
8 PM
9 PM
10 PM

DAY 75

FRIDAY

Top Three Tasks

1
2
3

Other Tasks

Schedule

7 AM
8 AM
9 AM
10 AM
11 AM
12 PM
1 PM
2 PM
3 PM
4 PM
5 PM
6 PM
7 PM
8 PM
9 PM
10 PM

DAY 76

SATURDAY _____ / ____

Top Three Tasks

1 _____

2 _____

3 _____

Other Tasks

_____
_____
_____
_____
_____
_____
_____
_____
_____
_____
_____
_____
_____

Schedule

7 AM _____

8 AM _____

9 AM _____

10 AM _____

11 AM _____

12 PM _____

1 PM _____

2 PM _____

3 PM _____

4 PM _____

5 PM _____

6 PM _____

7 PM _____

8 PM _____

9 PM _____

10 PM _____

DAY 77

Top Three Tasks

1
2
3

Other Tasks

Schedule

7 AM
8 AM
9 AM
10 AM
11 AM
12 PM
1 PM
2 PM
3 PM
4 PM
5 PM
6 PM
7 PM
8 PM
9 PM
10 PM

THIS WEEK'S GOALS

Starts _____ / _____   **Ends** _____ / _____

Top Three

① _____

② _____

③ _____

Other Goals

_____

_____

_____

_____

_____

_____

_____

_____

_____

_____

_____

_____

_____

_____

DAY 78

MONDAY

Top Three Tasks

1 ....

2 ....

3 ....

....

Other Tasks

....
....
....
....
....
....
....
....
....
....
....
....
....
....
....
....

Schedule

7 AM ....

8 AM ....

9 AM ....

10 AM ....

11 AM ....

12 PM ....

1 PM ....

2 PM ....

3 PM ....

4 PM ....

5 PM ....

6 PM ....

7 PM ....

8 PM ....

9 PM ....

10 PM ....

DAY 79

TUESDAY   /

Top Three Tasks

1

2

3

Other Tasks

Schedule

7 AM

8 AM

9 AM

10 AM

11 AM

12 PM

1 PM

2 PM

3 PM

4 PM

5 PM

6 PM

7 PM

8 PM

9 PM

10 PM

DAY 80

WEDNESDAY

Top Three Tasks

1
2
3

Other Tasks

Schedule

7 AM
8 AM
9 AM
10 AM
11 AM
12 PM
1 PM
2 PM
3 PM
4 PM
5 PM
6 PM
7 PM
8 PM
9 PM
10 PM

DAY 81

Top Three Tasks

1 _____

2 _____

3 _____

_____

Other Tasks

_____
_____
_____
_____
_____
_____
_____
_____
_____
_____
_____
_____
_____
_____
_____
_____

Schedule

7 AM _____

8 AM _____

9 AM _____

10 AM _____

11 AM _____

12 PM _____

1 PM _____

2 PM _____

3 PM _____

4 PM _____

5 PM _____

6 PM _____

7 PM _____

8 PM _____

9 PM _____

10 PM _____

SHOW YOUR PAYCHECK WHO'S BOSS!

FRIDAY

DAY 82

Top Three Tasks

1 ....

2 ....

3 ....

Other Tasks

....
....
....
....
....
....
....
....
....
....
....
....
....
....

Schedule

7 AM ....

8 AM ....

9 AM ....

10 AM ....

11 AM ....

12 PM ....

1 PM ....

2 PM ....

3 PM ....

4 PM ....

5 PM ....

6 PM ....

7 PM ....

8 PM ....

9 PM ....

10 PM ....

DAY 83

SATURDAY _____ / ____

Top Three Tasks

1
2
3

Other Tasks

Schedule

7 AM
8 AM
9 AM
10 AM
11 AM
12 PM
1 PM
2 PM
3 PM
4 PM
5 PM
6 PM
7 PM
8 PM
9 PM
10 PM

DAY 84

SUNDAY

Top Three Tasks

1

2

3

Other Tasks

Schedule

7 AM

8 AM

9 AM

10 AM

11 AM

12 PM

1 PM

2 PM

3 PM

4 PM

5 PM

6 PM

7 PM

8 PM

9 PM

10 PM

THIS WEEK'S GOALS

Starts _____   **Ends** _____

Top Three

① _____

② _____

③ _____

Other Goals

_____
_____
_____
_____
_____
_____
_____
_____
_____
_____
_____
_____
_____
_____
_____
_____

DAY 85

| | / | MONDAY |

Top Three Tasks

1 _____

2 _____

3 _____
_____

Other Tasks

_____
_____
_____
_____
_____
_____
_____
_____
_____
_____
_____
_____
_____
_____
_____

Schedule

7 AM _____
8 AM _____
9 AM _____
10 AM _____
11 AM _____
12 PM _____
1 PM _____
2 PM _____
3 PM _____
4 PM _____
5 PM _____
6 PM _____
7 PM _____
8 PM _____
9 PM _____
10 PM _____

DAY 86

TUESDAY /

Top Three Tasks

1

2

3

Other Tasks

Schedule

7 AM

8 AM

9 AM

10 AM

11 AM

12 PM

1 PM

2 PM

3 PM

4 PM

5 PM

6 PM

7 PM

8 PM

9 PM

10 PM

SHOW YOUR PAYCHECK WHO'S BOSS!

DAY 87

WEDNESDAY

Top Three Tasks

1
2
3

Other Tasks

Schedule

7 AM
8 AM
9 AM
10 AM
11 AM
12 PM
1 PM
2 PM
3 PM
4 PM
5 PM
6 PM
7 PM
8 PM
9 PM
10 PM

DAY 88

THURSDAY _____ / _____

Top Three Tasks

1 _____

2 _____

3 _____

_____

Other Tasks

_____
_____
_____
_____
_____
_____
_____
_____
_____
_____
_____
_____
_____
_____
_____
_____

Schedule

7 AM
8 AM
9 AM
10 AM
11 AM
12 PM
1 PM
2 PM
3 PM
4 PM
5 PM
6 PM
7 PM
8 PM
9 PM
10 PM

DAY 89

FRIDAY

Top Three Tasks

1

2

3

Other Tasks

Schedule

7 AM

8 AM

9 AM

10 AM

11 AM

12 PM

1 PM

2 PM

3 PM

4 PM

5 PM

6 PM

7 PM

8 PM

9 PM

10 PM

DAY 90

SATURDAY _____ / ____

Top Three Tasks

1 _____

2 _____

3 _____

Other Tasks

_____
_____
_____
_____
_____
_____
_____
_____
_____
_____
_____
_____
_____
_____
_____
_____

Schedule

7 AM
8 AM
9 AM
10 AM
11 AM
12 PM
1 PM
2 PM
3 PM
4 PM
5 PM
6 PM
7 PM
8 PM
9 PM
10 PM

DAY 91

SUNDAY

Top Three Tasks

1
2
3

Other Tasks

Schedule

7 AM
8 AM
9 AM
10 AM
11 AM
12 PM
1 PM
2 PM
3 PM
4 PM
5 PM
6 PM
7 PM
8 PM
9 PM
10 PM

THIS WEEK'S GOALS

Starts _____ / _____   **Ends** _____ / _____

Top Three

① _____

② _____

③ _____

Other Goals

DAY 92

_____ / ___ MONDAY

Top Three Tasks

1 ....

2 ....

3 ....

Other Tasks

....

....

....

....

....

....

....

....

....

....

....

....

....

....

....

....

Schedule

7 AM ....

8 AM ....

9 AM ....

10 AM ....

11 AM ....

12 PM ....

1 PM ....

2 PM ....

3 PM ....

4 PM ....

5 PM ....

6 PM ....

7 PM ....

8 PM ....

9 PM ....

10 PM ....

DAY 93

TUESDAY _____ / ____

Top Three Tasks

1 _____

2 _____

3 _____

Other Tasks

_____
_____
_____
_____
_____
_____
_____
_____
_____
_____
_____
_____
_____
_____

Schedule

7 AM
8 AM
9 AM
10 AM
11 AM
12 PM
1 PM
2 PM
3 PM
4 PM
5 PM
6 PM
7 PM
8 PM
9 PM
10 PM

DAY 94

WEDNESDAY

Top Three Tasks

1
2
3

Other Tasks

Schedule

7 AM
8 AM
9 AM
10 AM
11 AM
12 PM
1 PM
2 PM
3 PM
4 PM
5 PM
6 PM
7 PM
8 PM
9 PM
10 PM

DAY 95

THURSDAY _____ / _____

Top Three Tasks

1 _____

2 _____

3 _____

Other Tasks

_____
_____
_____
_____
_____
_____
_____
_____
_____
_____
_____
_____
_____
_____

Schedule

7 AM _____
8 AM _____
9 AM _____
10 AM _____
11 AM _____
12 PM _____
1 PM _____
2 PM _____
3 PM _____
4 PM _____
5 PM _____
6 PM _____
7 PM _____
8 PM _____
9 PM _____
10 PM _____

DAY 96

FRIDAY

Top Three Tasks	Schedule
1	7 AM
2	8 AM
	9 AM
3	10 AM
	11 AM
Other Tasks	12 PM
	1 PM
	2 PM
	3 PM
	4 PM
	5 PM
	6 PM
	7 PM
	8 PM
	9 PM
	10 PM

DAY 97

SATURDAM /

Top Three Tasks

1

2

3

Other Tasks

Schedule

7 AM

8 AM

9 AM

10 AM

11 AM

12 PM

1 PM

2 PM

3 PM

4 PM

5 PM

6 PM

7 PM

8 PM

9 PM

10 PM

DAY 98

SUNDAY

Top Three Tasks

1

2

3

Other Tasks

Schedule

7 AM

8 AM

9 AM

10 AM

11 AM

12 PM

1 PM

2 PM

3 PM

4 PM

5 PM

6 PM

7 PM

8 PM

9 PM

10 PM

THIS WEEK'S GOALS

Starts _____   **Ends** _____

Top Three

① _____

② _____

③ _____

Other Goals

_____
_____
_____
_____
_____
_____
_____
_____
_____
_____
_____
_____
_____
_____
_____
_____

MONDAY

DAY 99

Top Three Tasks

1

2

3

Other Tasks

Schedule

7 AM

8 AM

9 AM

10 AM

11 AM

12 PM

1 PM

2 PM

3 PM

4 PM

5 PM

6 PM

7 PM

8 PM

9 PM

10 PM

DAY 100

TUESDAY _____ / _____

Top Three Tasks

1 _____

2 _____

3 _____

Other Tasks

_____
_____
_____
_____
_____
_____
_____
_____
_____
_____
_____
_____
_____
_____
_____

Schedule

7 AM _____

8 AM _____

9 AM _____

10 AM _____

11 AM _____

12 PM _____

1 PM _____

2 PM _____

3 PM _____

4 PM _____

5 PM _____

6 PM _____

7 PM _____

8 PM _____

9 PM _____

10 PM _____

WEDNESDAY

**DAY
101**

Top Three Tasks

1
2
3

Other Tasks

Schedule

7 AM
8 AM
9 AM
10 AM
11 AM
12 PM
1 PM
2 PM
3 PM
4 PM
5 PM
6 PM
7 PM
8 PM
9 PM
10 PM

DAY 102

THURSDAY _____ / _____

Top Three Tasks

1 _____

2 _____

3 _____

_____

Other Tasks

_____
_____
_____
_____
_____
_____
_____
_____
_____
_____
_____
_____
_____

Schedule

7 AM _____
8 AM _____
9 AM _____
10 AM _____
11 AM _____
12 PM _____
1 PM _____
2 PM _____
3 PM _____
4 PM _____
5 PM _____
6 PM _____
7 PM _____
8 PM _____
9 PM _____
10 PM _____

DAY 103

FRIDAY

Top Three Tasks

1 ....

2 ....

3 ....

Other Tasks

....

....

....

....

....

....

....

....

....

....

....

....

....

....

....

....

Schedule

7 AM ....

8 AM ....

9 AM ....

10 AM ....

11 AM ....

12 PM ....

1 PM ....

2 PM ....

3 PM ....

4 PM ....

5 PM ....

6 PM ....

7 PM ....

8 PM ....

9 PM ....

10 PM ....

DAY 104

SATURDAY _____ / _____

Top Three Tasks	Schedule
1 _____	7 AM
2 _____	8 AM
3 _____	9 AM
	10 AM
	11 AM
Other Tasks	12 PM
	1 PM
	2 PM
	3 PM
	4 PM
	5 PM
	6 PM
	7 PM
	8 PM
	9 PM
	10 PM

 SUNDAY

DAY 105

Top Three Tasks

1
2
3

Other Tasks

Schedule

7 AM
8 AM
9 AM
10 AM
11 AM
12 PM
1 PM
2 PM
3 PM
4 PM
5 PM
6 PM
7 PM
8 PM
9 PM
10 PM

Dear Single Mom or Dad,

Thank you so much for taking the time to read *Show Your Paycheck Who's Boss*. I truly hope that this book helps you. I believe that if you have a plan, you can do anything you put your mind to.

I encourage you to use the planners. Fold down the corners of the pages. Write notes all over the pages. Show them to your friends, and accountability partner.

If you have questions, or want to reach out to me, feel free to contact me at www.MotinaBooks.com. I would love to hear about your single parent journey.

You are not alone.

Diane

Glossary

401K	This is an employer sponsored retirement plan. Your contribution is deducted from your paycheck before taxes are taken out. In most cases, your employer will match up to a specific percent.
529 Plan	This is an education savings account that you can open yourself. You make your own contributions, so they're post-tax. As long as you use the money in this account for educational purposes, the money earned is tax free.
Accountability Partner	This is the person who you can go to when you're feeling stuck. They'll keep you on the right track, and make sure you don't fall off the wagon.
Allowance	Money that is given to someone just because they're breathing.
Budget	The written account of how much money is coming in, and how much is going out. It lists every payment that is due each month, and when it's due.
Child Support	The court-ordered amount of money that is paid every month by the non-custodial parent to the custodial parent. This money is used to provide food, clothing, and shelter for the children.

Commission	Money that is earned by performing a job or task.
Cosign	The promise to a lender that if the primary borrower fails to make payments on a loan, YOU will make those payments. The cosigner is as just as responsible for making these payments as the primary borrower is.
Credit Report	The annual report provided by each of the three credit bureaus. This report lists your outstanding debts.
Custodial Parent	The parent with the who has the majority of parenting time for the children.
Domain Name	This is the name of your website.
Dual-Credit Classes	These are classes students take in high school that count for both high school and college credit. These are FANTASTIC!
Emergency Fund	This is the money you keep just for emergencies. New shoes and birthdays are not emergencies.
Envelope System	The magical cash system that helps keep you on your budget. Write the name of each spending category on the envelope. Place the designated amount of money in that envelope. If the envelope is empty, you can't spend anything in that category.
Equity	The amount of money in your home, between the amount that you owe, and the amount that you could sell it for.

FICO Score	This is your credit score. It's determined by multiple factors. It ranges from 300 to 850.
Gross Income	Your income before deductions are taken out of your paycheck.
IRA	This is a retirement fund you open on your own. Contributions are pre-tax, so they can be deducted from your taxes. The growth on this account is tax-deferred.
Negative Equity	If you owe more than your home is worth, and you won't be able to make money from it when you sell it, you have negative equity in your home.
Net Income	Your income after deductions are taken out of your paycheck. Your take-home pay.
Non-Custodial Parent	The parent who makes the child support payment to the other parent. Typically has a bit less parenting time.
Payday Loan	A short-term, high-interest loan that no one should ever take out. It's based on your paycheck.
Roth	A 401K or IRA retirement savings plan based on post-tax contributions. This account grows tax-free.
Title Loan	A short-term, high-interest loan that no one should ever take out. It's based on your car title.

Top Ten Financial Tips for Young People

10. Pay off your credit card every month.

Having a credit card today is kind of a necessary evil. It can help you build a credit history, which is good, but if you don't use it responsibly it can get you into lots of trouble. A credit history is important for insurance rates, renting an apartment or even finding a job. A good way to build your credit is to pay for your cell phone bill using the card, and paying it off EVERY SINGLE MONTH. Don't buy a new phone with the card – just pay for your monthly cell phone bill. It's very easy to get in over your head with credit cards. Many people have thousands of dollars in credit card debt, and it's very hard to pay that off.

9. Never "rent" furniture, appliances or electronics from a rent-to-own store front.

You shouldn't have to rent furniture, appliances or electronics from a rent-to-own store. The interest rates on these items are astronomical! If you need furniture, appliances, or electronics, save the money and buy it.

8. Never ask another person to co-sign a loan for you.

If you try to borrow money from a bank, and they won't lend it to you without another person (who has good credit) signing the loan application, then you shouldn't be borrowing money. If you stop paying on the loan, the co-signer will be completely responsible.

7. Never co-sign a loan for another person.

For the same reason that you should not ask another person to co-sign a loan for you, you should never co-sign for another person – not even a family member.

6. Never take out a title loan.

A title loan is a short-term loan where you put up the title of your car as collateral. The interest rates range from 212% to 911%.

5. Never take out a payday loan.

Payday loans are marketed as "short-term, one-time helpful loans." They are actually a trap that is very difficult to escape. Interest rates are similar to title loans – 212% to 911%.

4. Make sure you have a rainy day fund in the bank.

If you have a rainy day fund of three to six months of your monthly expenses in the bank, you won't need a credit card or any other kind of loan when you need to fix your car, or pay for any other unexpected emergency.

3. Start saving for retirement early.

If you start investing in a retirement account (such as an IRA or 401K) when you're in your early twenties, you will be SET by the time you're ready to retire.

2. Live on a written budget.

Spend your money on paper, before you spend it for real. That way you'll know how much you're spending in various categories.

1. Spend less than you make.

Diane Windsor - 2012

PAGE 289

About the Author

Diane Windsor is an author and small publisher in beautiful North Texas. She spent many years as the leader of the largest single parent support group in Collin County.

9 781945 060687